Praise for *Abraham*

"I can think of few things that the contemporary church needs to recover as much as the ancient practice of lectio divina. *Abraham* is a welcome contribution in this direction. Abraham is central to the biblical narrative and it is ~ ~d to see Binz drawing our attention not only to the Abr~~ also to Abraham in other parts of the Old ar~~ book is rightly on the biblical text itself, a~~ ~sh us back to the text to listen for God's a~~ ~itten and accessible tool will assist readers

—Craig Barthol~~ ~*ne Drama of Scripture*

"Lectio divina is the perfect practice for studying the life, struggles, and hopes of Abraham and his dynamic significance for the faith and outreach of each one of us! Binz has done a splendid job of introducing his readers to this practice and immersing them in it. I eagerly suggest this volume—and the entire series—as the basis for your next personal or group study."

—Marva J. Dawn, Regent College

"Lectio divina, despite its centuries-long use, is still little known outside of monastic and academic settings. Ancient-Future Bible Study has in mind to correct that historical defect in Christian piety. The quality of *Abraham*, the first volume in the series, bodes well for the whole project."

—Patrick Henry Reardon, author, *Creation and the Patriarchal Histories*

"A method of Bible study that has a long and celebrated history in the church is given renewed momentum with this book. Using the story of Abraham, as well as the New Testament writers' reinterpretation of elements of that story, Binz both introduces lay readers to this important biblical character and leads them through the five movements of lectio divina. The book will be a wonderful aid for the development of one's spiritual life."

—Dianne Bergant, CSA, Catholic Theological Union

"I heartily recommend *Abraham*, as it allows us to engage the story of the great patriarch through the extraordinary—and simple—means of lectio divina. It allows us to put down the commentaries and word studies and let the beautiful poignancy of the text seep into our souls, all with the aid of the Holy Spirit."

—Tony Jones, Solomon's Porch, Minneapolis; author,
The New Christians: Dispatches from the Emergent Frontier

Praise for Ancient-Future Bible Study

"At their recent Synod the world's Catholic bishops recommended lectio divina to all Christ's disciples, for prayerfully reading and making God's Word one's spiritual nourishment follows well-trod paths in the Christian tradition. Binz guides us on these paths in his Ancient-Future Bible Study series. I am pleased to recommend this project with enthusiasm."

—Terrence Prendergast, SJ, Archbishop of Ottawa

"Ancient-Future Bible Study brings a centuries-old approach to Scripture and prayer into the twenty-first century, providing sound commentary, thoughtful insights, and meaningful suggestions for personal reflection and meditation. Binz invites us to open our minds and hearts to the transforming power of God's Word. Under his guidance, the wisdom of the Bible comes vividly to life."

—Carl McColman, author, *The Big Book of Christian Mysticism*

"This series is a wonderful gift for the church in late modernity. In an era of twittered attention, we have inculcated all sorts of bad reading habits that we then bring to Scripture. The Ancient-Future Bible Study prescribes a counter-formative regimen: the personal and communal practice of lectio divina or 'sacred reading.' For some this will be a strange, new practice; but it will quickly feel as natural as breathing."

—James K. A. Smith, Calvin College; author, *Desiring the Kingdom: Worship, Worldview, and Cultural Formation*

"Binz has a knack for popularizing the Bible. His latest series, Ancient-Future Bible Study, demonstrates once more his ability to give people sound guidance as they read the Bible. I am happy to warmly recommend this modern application of the ancient method of lectio divina centered on fascinating characters from the Old and New Testaments."

—Fr. Ronald D. Witherup, author, *The Bible Companion*

"Binz has undertaken the important project of leading non-professional but committed readers of the Bible into a spiritually enlivening encounter with the biblical text through engagement with some of the fascinating characters who people its pages. Anyone yearning to pray the biblical text will find this series a useful companion."

—Sandra M. Schneiders, Jesuit School of Theology

ΛΝCIEΝT-FUTURE BIBLE STUDY

ABRAHAM

Father of All Believers

STEPHEN J. BINZ

a division of Baker Publishing Group
Grand Rapids, Michigan

© 2011 by Stephen J. Binz

Published by Brazos Press
a division of Baker Publishing Group
P.O. Box 6287, Grand Rapids, MI 49516-6287
www.brazospress.com

Printed in the United States of America

Library of Congress Cataloging-in-Publication Data
Binz, Stephen J., 1955–
    Abraham : father of all believers / Stephen J. Binz.
        p.   cm. — (Ancient-future Bible study)
    ISBN 978-1-58743-277-4 (pbk.)
    1. Abraham (Biblical patriarch—Textbooks. 2. Patriarchs (Bible—Biography—Textbooks. 3. Bible. O.T. Genesis—Textbooks. I. Title. II. Series.
BS580.A3B46 2011
222′.11092—dc22   2010021406

Scripture is taken from the New Revised Standard Version of the Bible, copyright © 1989, by the Division of Christian Education of the National Council of the Churches of Christ in the United States of America. Used by permission. All rights reserved.

Some content from "Overview of Ancient-Future Bible Study" originally appeared in Stephen J. Binz, *Conversing with God in Scripture: A Contemporary Approach to Lectio Divina* (Ijamsville, MD: The Word Among Us Press, 2008).

11   12   13   14   15   16   17   7   6   5   4   3   2   1

Contents

Acknowledgments

For the past several years my work has focused on making connections between ancient practices and contemporary experiences. My speaking, writing, and counseling under the umbrella of Bridge-Building Opportunities has emphasized the link between past and present, East and West, time-honored tradition and progressive renewal in the fields of biblical theology, Christian spirituality, and personal growth.

When I discovered the mission of Brazos Press, I felt that I had found a new home. By its own definition, Brazos Press is "staked on the discernment that while various existing Christian categories (liberal and conservative, mainline and evangelical, even Catholic and Protestant) prove increasingly unserviceable, there is at the same time occurring a robust renewal of classical, orthodox Christianity across many of the old lines or borders." This is a publisher that is eager to cross boundaries, build bridges, and extend the vital roots of the ancient Christian tradition into the twenty-first century.

I am grateful to Jim Kinney, associate publisher and editorial director of Baker Academic and Brazos Press, for supporting my work. Lisa Ann Cockrel, editor for this series, has masterfully guided these books through the editorial process and improved this work with her many ideas. I also appreciate the skillful work of Lisa Beth Anderson, Rodney Clapp, Steve Ayers, BJ Heyboer, Jeremy Wells, Caitlin Mackenzie, and the whole Brazos team for their efforts to refine and promote this project.

The term "Ancient-Future" seems to perfectly express the bridge between ancient wisdom and future possibilities that I want to create in this series. The term is applied in a number of other spheres to emphasize a blending of tradition and innovation. In the arts, ancient-future music and dance is created through fusing centuries-old traditions with contemporary genres and technology. By learning from the world's great traditions and ancient practices, artists create cross-cultural expressions that are richly profound yet also widely appealing.

I am particularly indebted to the work of the late Robert Webber, many of whose titles use the term "Ancient-Future" to express his mission of drawing wisdom from the past and translating those insights into the present and future life of the church, its faith, worship, ministry, and spirituality. In his own words: "My argument is that the era of the early church (AD 100–500), and particularly the second century, contains insights which evangelicals need to recover." This series resonates with his outstanding work and hopefully, in some small way, will honor his memory and continue his vision.

Finally, I am grateful to all my friends and colleagues in the field of biblical studies and to all pastors, lay ministers, and church volunteers who are dedicated to an anciently rooted and forward-looking Christianity. Particularly I want to express my appreciation to my wife Pamela, a professor of music, for the loving support and inspiration she constantly offers to me.

Welcome to Ancient-Future Bible Study

Ancient-Future Bible Study unites contemporary study of the Bible with an experience of the church's most ancient way of reading Scripture, *lectio divina*. By combining the old and the new in a fertile synthesis, this study helps modern people encounter the *sacra pagina*, the inspired text, as God intends it for the church. Through solid historical and literary study and the time-honored practice of lectio divina, the mind and the heart are brought into an experience of God through a careful and prayerful reading of the biblical texts.

As the Word of its divine author, the Bible is not just a literary anthology of ancient texts; it is inspired literature addressed to God's people. God intends the sacred texts to move from our heads to the depths of our hearts and to form us as a new people living in God's reign. Ancient-Future Bible Study guides readers to listen to Scripture within the tradition and scholarship of the church in order to unleash its life-changing potential.

The ancient art of lectio divina is rooted in the Jewish tradition of Jesus, and it was nourished through the desert spirituality of the early centuries, the patristic writers of the ancient church, and the monastic tradition through the ages. In our day, lectio divina is experiencing a worldwide revival as Christians are returning to age-old wisdom to experience the Scriptures in a deeper and more complete way.

As you experience Ancient-Future Bible Study, you will realize how the church's long tradition of biblical study, reflection, prayer, discernment, and contemplative action can enrich your discipleship. You will learn how to dispose yourself to be formed by the Word of God as you join with the array of men and women through the ages whose lives have been transformed by that same living Word.

Reasons for Studying the Bible

Most often people study the Bible for one of three reasons. First, they study for information and knowledge. This usually includes a search for historical facts, doctrinal truths, and moral guidance. Second, they study to find advice for solving a personal need or getting through a life crisis. This usually involves seeking out lists of specific passages that speak to the particular needs of the moment. Third, they study so they can defend their faith and witness to others. This usually consists of choosing selected passages to remember and quote, so they can argue for a particular approach to faith or help lead others toward the truth. While all of these objectives can lead to good results, their accomplishments are always limited and partial.

The most complete reason for studying Scripture is for the purpose of encountering the living God through the sacred text. This divine encounter leads not just to more information and advice but to a deeply rooted transformation of life. The inspired Word evokes a spiritual transformation within the lives of those who allow God's Word to do its true work, urging us to personal growth in Christ and fuller discipleship.

For Scripture to have its deepest effects in us we must approach the text with humility, reverence, and expectation. As we receive its revelation and understand its truth, Scripture has the ability to gradually change our minds and mold our hearts. Unlike any other literature, the words of the Bible can renew our lives when we approach the text as an encounter with its divine author.

The Indwelling of the Holy Spirit

The Bible was written under the inspiration of the Holy Spirit. God's "breathing in," acting in union with the human authors of the texts, makes the Scriptures the Word of the living God. Because God is the primary author of the Bible, we can be assured that the texts have a power that transcends that of any other spiritual reading.

God's inspiration of the biblical books does not refer only to a past reality, to the historical time in which the biblical authors were guided to write the texts. Rather, the work of God's Spirit is an ongoing reality within the inspired books. The sacred texts remain inspired; they are forever permeated with divine breath and are filled now with the Spirit of God.

This understanding of the Spirit's enduring and ongoing presence in the biblical texts is the foundation of lectio divina. Through the Holy Spirit, God addresses his Word to us here and now through the ancient text. Because of the indwelling Spirit, the Word is alive and has the power to transform us. The Word of God is charged with creative power to change and renew us from within.

The Movements of Lectio Divina

Lectio divina (LEK-tsee-oh dih-VEEN-ah) is best translated, though incompletely, as "sacred reading." Its revitalization, like the renewal of other spiritual practices from the early church, is becoming a means of deep spiritual growth for people today. Lectio divina helps us return to the most ancient understanding of the sacredness of the inspired text. The Bible is not like a textbook, used for looking up factual documentation, nor is it like a manual, describing a how-to method for solving problems. Rather, it is a means of forming our life in God and joining us to the story of God's people.

The process of lectio divina appeals not only to our minds but also to our imaginations and feelings. We seek to understand and experience Scripture as a real communication, as God personally addressing us. In practicing lectio divina, we get caught up in the literature and learn to love the text itself; we read it reflectively, lingering over it, and let it reach the depths of our hearts. We let go of our own agenda and expectations, gradually opening ourselves to what God wants us to experience through the sacred page.

There is no single method for the practice of lectio divina. It is not a rigid step-by-step system for encountering God in biblical passages. The spiritual masters of the early church distrusted methods of prayer and spiritual practice that were too rigidly defined, wishing instead to cultivate the freedom necessary to respond to the Spirit's promptings. Lectio divina aims toward a holistic experience of Scripture, incorporating our intellects, feelings, and actions.

Ancient-Future Bible Study incorporates five "movements." Comparable to the movements in a classical work of music, each movement has its own characteristics and can even be practiced independently of the others. There is plenty of room for personal interpretation within the tradition. Individually and together, lectio, meditatio, oratio, contemplatio, and operatio contribute to the full experience of lectio divina.

Pronunciation Guide

Lectio—LEK-tsee-oh
Meditatio—meh-dih-TAH-tsee-oh
Oratio—oh-RAH-tsee-oh
Contemplatio—con-tem-PLAH-tsee-oh
Operatio—oh-peh-RAH-tsee-oh

Lectio—*Reading the Text with a Listening Ear*

Lectio is more than ordinary reading. It might best be described as listening deeply—what St. Benedict in the sixth century described as hearing "with the ear of our heart." This listening requires that we try to receive God's Word with as little prejudgment as possible, as if we were hearing it for the first time. Lectio urges us to create a space within us for the new wisdom and understanding God wants to give us through the sacred page.

Saint Ambrose in the fourth century urged readers to avoid the tendency to read large passages in haste: "We should read not in agitation, but in calm; not hurriedly, but slowly, a few words at a time, pausing in attentive reflection. . . . Then the readers will experience their ability to enkindle the ardor of prayer." We might even consider returning to the ancient practice of reading texts aloud in order to instill within ourselves the sense of reading Scripture as a deep listening.

The essential question to ask in this first movement is, "What does the text say and what does it mean?" The Jewish rabbis and the church's patristic writers show us that there is no clear distinction between studying and praying Scripture. The more we come to understand the text with our minds, the more we are capable of being changed by the text. Wrestling with the text and seeking to comprehend its meaning is an important part of encountering God there and being changed by that encounter.

Once we've read the text slowly and carefully, Ancient-Future Bible Study invites us to learn from the commentary that follows the biblical passage. This too is part of listening to the text, only here we listen with the understanding of the church and with some basic insights of biblical scholarship. This listening to the text, with its multiple layers of meaning and rich history of interpretation, forms the foundation on which we experience the subsequent movements of lectio divina. We do what we can to make sure our reading of the text is faithful and true, so that we don't reduce God's revelation to our own imaginary constructions. On this firm basis, we construct the process of prayerfully encountering God's Word.

We might read the text as literature, looking at its words, metaphors, images, and characters. We could look at its structure and its literary form—is it poetry, parable, history, proverb, legal code, epic, or apocalypse? We should realize that God's truth is expressed in a variety of types of literature, each type expressing truth in a different way. The more we can comprehend something of the original historical, cultural, literary, and religious context of the passage, the better we will be able to probe all the potential the text can offer us.

In lectio, the words of Scripture become the means of God speaking to us. As God's Spirit guided the human authors to express the truth that God wished to entrust to the Scriptures, God also guides us through that same Spirit as we read the Bible as God's Word to us.

Meditatio—*Reflecting on the Meaning and Message of the Text*

The question to ask in this movement is, "What does the text say to me and mean to me?" Meditatio aims to bring the biblical passage into the sphere of my own life as I seek to understand how the Scripture passage speaks to me today.

Though there is a wide gap of time, language, and culture between the world of the biblical writers and our own world, meditatio bridges that gap. By reflecting on the text as well as on our own experiences, thoughts, challenges, and questions, we can grow in our understanding that God is speaking personally to us through the scriptural text. This reflection forms connections between the text of yesterday and the today of our lives.

Ancient-Future Bible Study stimulates meditatio through the use of questions for reflection. These questions encourage a deeper and more personal consideration of the text. They challenge the reader to create a dialogue between the ancient text and life today. As the Word of God, the Bible has a richness of meaning that can be discovered in every age and every culture. It has a particular message that can be received by everyone who listens to God's Word in the context of daily experiences and in the same Spirit in which it was written.

The more we meditate on God's Word, the more it seeps into our lives and saturates our thoughts and feelings. Meditatio allows the dynamic Word of God to so penetrate our lives that it truly infuses our minds and hearts and we begin to embody its truth and its goodness.

Oratio—*Praying in Response to God's Word*

Careful lectio and reflective meditatio open the way for God to enter into our hearts and inflame them with the grace of his love. There, at the core of our being, we naturally want to respond to the One whose voice we have heard. Oratio is our prayerful response to God's Word.

Lectio divina is fundamentally a dialogue with God, a gentle oscillation between listening to God and responding to him in prayer. When we recognize that God has offered us a message that is unique to our own lives—an insight, a challenge, a comfort, a call—we arrive at the moment when we must ask ourselves, "Now what am I going to say in response to God?" This is the moment of prayer.

Oratio is not just any form of prayer. It is born from the experience of listening to God in Scripture. The biblical words we have heard and reflected on become the words of our prayer. The style and vocabulary of our prayer are enriched through the inspired words of the biblical tradition. Whether our oratio is an act of praise or thanksgiving, of petition or repentance, we pray in response to what we have heard. Our prayers no longer consist of mechanically repeated formulas. Rather, they resonate with the faith, hope, and love that animated the people of the Bible in their journey with God.

Ancient-Future Bible Study offers examples of this type of prayer. After each session of lectio and meditatio, we are encouraged to continue in intimate prayer to God, melding the words, images, and sentiments of the biblical text with personal thoughts, feelings, and desires arising from the heart.

Contemplatio—*Quietly Resting in God*

Both oratio and contemplatio are forms of prayer. Oratio is our active, word-filled prayer in response to God's Word. Contemplatio is prayer without words. It is the response to God that remains after words are no longer necessary or helpful. It is simply enjoying the experience of quietly being in God's presence.

Contemplatio requires that we let go of any effort to be in charge of the process. When we feel God drawing us into a deeper awareness of his divine presence, we gradually abandon our intellectual activity and let ourselves be wooed into God's embrace. We no longer have to think or reason, listen or speak. The experience resembles that of lovers holding each other in wordless silence or of a sleeping child resting in the arms of his or her mother.

Though we may think the movement of contemplatio is passive and uneventful, it is not. When we humbly expose our heart, the center of our being, to God, what happens within us during those moments is really not up to us. In contrast to the rapid, noisy communication of our technological world, quiet, receptive stillness is the atmosphere in which the most important communication occurs. God's grace is truly at work in those moments, and the Holy Spirit is changing us without our direct knowledge or understanding.

Operatio—*Faithful Witness in Daily Life*

After reading, reflecting, and praying over a scriptural passage, we should be impacted in a way that makes a difference in our daily lives. Operatio is our lived response to the biblical text. The question operatio calls forth from us is, "How can I live out the Word of God that I have heard in my heart?"

We cannot prayerfully read Scripture without being changed in some specific way. As we deepen our relationship with God through the movements of lectio divina, our actions become vehicles of his presence to others. We become channels of God's compassion and mercy, becoming "doers of the word, and not merely hearers" (James 1:22), bringing about God's loving purposes in our daily lives.

Contemplatio and operatio should not be totally distinct and separate. Their impulses grow together in the heart of one who prayerfully reads Scripture. Contemplatio does not separate us from the world, and operatio is not genuine unless it grows out of contemplative reflection. Apart from contemplatio, operatio could become superficial pragmatism.

The Bible should never be viewed as simply a collection of maxims to be put into practice. Rarely does Scripture offer us concrete details about what to do in specific situations. Our human reason and experience must always accompany our prayerful discernment as we decide how to live out the Word of God. Listening, reflection, prayer, and contemplation are all necessary components from which flows the operatio of Christian discipleship. Lectio divina helps us become contemplative activists and active contemplatives.

The Essence of Lectio Divina

The movements of lectio divina are more like the colors of a rainbow than clearly defined stages. They overlap, blending into one another, ebbing and flowing according to the rhythm of the divine Spirit and the human heart. The five movements used in Ancient-Future Bible Study are part of a rich tradition, though additional phases are sometimes found in other historical forms of the practice: studium (study), cogitatio (reflection), consolatio (comfort), discretio (discernment), deliberatio (decision making), compassio (compassion), and actio (action).

While the most ancient practice of lectio divina is not a rigid system of biblical reflection, nor does its method require any particular steps, there are a few characteristics that identify the authentic practice of lectio divina:

‡ *Lectio divina is a personal encounter with God through Scripture.* The text itself is a gateway to God. Through the inspired Scripture, we meet the God who loves us and desires our response.

‡ *Lectio divina establishes a dialogue between the reader of Scripture and God.* The attentive reader listens to God through the text and responds to God in heartfelt prayer. The heart of lectio divina is this gentle conversation with God.

‡ *Lectio divina creates a heart-to-heart intimacy with God.* In the Bible, the heart is a person's innermost core, the place from which one's deepest longings, motivations, decisions, memories, and desires arise. The prayerful reader responds to God's Word with the whole heart and thereby grows in a relationship with God at the deepest level of intimacy.

‡ *Lectio divina leads to contemplation and action.* There is a moment in all true love that leads to a level of communication too deep for words. Prayerful reading inevitably leads to that deepest form of communication with God, which is loving silence. In addition, all true love must be expressed in action. Eventually words become inadequate, and love must be demonstrated in deeds arising from a changed heart.

The Word of God and its power to change us are gifts from God that we must accept into our lives. In order to receive the gift of divine intimacy, we must create the necessary conditions within us. Openheartedness, faithfulness, and expectation will enable us to more readily listen and receive. The more we remove the obstacles in the way—our inner resistance, our fear of intimacy, our impatient awareness of time, our desire to control the process, and our self-concern—the more we can expect Scripture to transform our lives.

Sometimes the changes are remarkable; more often they are subtle. We gradually become aware that the fruit of studying the Bible is the fruit of the Spirit: "love, joy, peace, patience, kindness, generosity, faithfulness, gentleness, and self-control" (Gal. 5:22–23). When we begin to notice this fruit in the way we live each day, we will know that the Word of God is working within us.

Your Personal Practice of Ancient-Future Bible Study

‡ This study is designed to provide maximum flexibility so that you can make lectio divina a regular part of your life according to your circum-

stances. If you are able to make the time in your daily schedule, you will want to reflect on one chapter each day. If not, you may select three weekdays to read three chapters per week. Or if your weekends are more leisurely, you may choose to reflect on two chapters per weekend.

‡ Reading Plan #1—30 days/5 weeks
  • Engage six lessons per week

‡ Reading Plan #2—60 days/10 weeks
  • Engage three lessons per week

‡ Reading Plan #3—90 days/15 weeks
  • Engage two lessons per weekend

‡ Whatever pace you choose for your practice of lectio divina, try to find a regular time during the day that can become a pattern for you. Choose a quiet and comfortable place where you will be undisturbed during the time of your lectio divina.

‡ During your regular time for lectio divina, try to rid yourself of as many distractions as possible. Before you begin reading the Bible, take time to call upon the Holy Spirit for guidance. Light a candle, ring a chime, kiss the Bible, or do some other action that will designate these moments as sacred time.

‡ Read the biblical text slowly and carefully. Read the passage in another translation, if you wish, to help your understanding. Don't hesitate to mark up this book with highlights, underlining, circles, or whatever will help you pay attention and remember the text and commentary.

‡ Follow the movements of lectio divina outlined in each section. Realize that this is only a tentative guide for the more important movements of God's Spirit within you. Write out your responses to the questions provided. The questions following the lectio are objective questions synthesizing your reading of the text and commentary. Those under meditatio are more personal questions, requiring thoughtful reflection. Try also to write comments on the sections of oratio, contemplatio, and operatio, according to the suggestions provided. The very act of writ-

ing will help you clarify your thoughts, bring new insights, and amplify your understanding.

‡ Approach your lectio divina with expectancy, trusting that God will indeed work deeply within you through his Word. Through this experience, know that you are placing yourself within a long procession of God's people through the ages who have allowed themselves to be transformed through lectio divina.

‡ Finally, try to be accountable to at least one other person for your regular practice of lectio divina. Tell a spouse, friend, spiritual director, or minister about your experience in order to receive their encouragement and affirmation.

Bringing Ancient-Future Bible Study to Churches

Throughout the history of salvation, God's Word has been directed first and foremost to a community, not just to individuals. The people of Israel, the community of disciples, and the early church were the recipients of God's self-communication expressed in the Scriptures. For this reason, studying the Bible in the context of a community of faith can deepen and enrich our individual experience.

Churches and other faith communities may choose to adopt Ancient-Future Bible Study and encourage its use in a variety of ways. Since this Bible study is ideally suited both for personal use by individuals and for communal practice, congregations are able to respect the many ways people desire to make Scripture a priority in their lives. By encouraging an array of options for participation, churches will increase the number of people in the congregation who are making reading and reflection on the Bible a regular part of their lives in Christ.

Collatio—The Communal Practice of Lectio Divina

The ancient term for the communal practice of lectio divina is collatio (coh-LAH-tsee-oh), a term that originally meant "a bringing together, interchange, or discussion." Its aim is building up a spiritual community around the Word of God. Collatio began in an age when books were rare and precious. Today, when everyone may have their own Bible, collatio may be practiced in many different ways.

Here are some ways of building up a faith community with Ancient-Future Bible Study:

‡ Offer this study to people who want to participate only on their own. Respect the fact that many people don't have the time or desire to gather with others. Instead they can be encouraged to read and reflect on their own with the prayerful support of the whole community.

‡ Promote the formation of informal groups made up of family, friends, neighbors, or work associates.

‡ Facilitate usage of the study through online communities or social networks. Online group members might want to commit themselves to sending an email or text message to the group offering their insights after reflecting on each Scripture passage.

‡ Set up small groups that meet regularly at church facilities or in homes. These groups may meet at different times throughout the week to offer convenient options for people in different circumstances. Groups could be made up of people with obvious connections: young adults, retired seniors, parents with young children, professionals, couples, etc. These groupings may encourage a deeper level of personal reflection among members.

Biblical reading and reflection on a regular basis is an important part of Christian discipleship. Every member of our congregations should be encouraged to make Bible reading and reflection a regular part of their lives. This is best accomplished when pastoral leadership promotes this practice and when people are personally invited to participate. When practicing lectio divina within a community of faith, we learn to place our own lives into the story of God's people throughout the ages.

Further Help for Groups

‡ Additional information for facilitating small groups with Ancient-Future Bible Study may be found starting on page 163 of this book.

‡ Since Ancient-Future Bible Study is divided into units of six lessons, motivated groups may choose to study five lessons per week on their own, with a weekly group session discussing insights from the daily lessons and practicing the sixth lesson of the week in the group.

‡ Groups with less daily time to study may divide the six lessons in half, choosing to study two lessons per week on their own, with a weekly group session discussing insights from the daily lessons and practicing the third lesson of the week in the group.

‡ The practice of lectio divina for each lesson will take about thirty minutes for an individual. Those who wish to spend extended time in reflection and prayer should allow for more time. The group session, using the suggestions at the back of this book, will take about ninety minutes.

‡ Additional information about Ancient-Future Bible Study, with descriptions of published and upcoming studies, may be found online at www .brazospress.com/ancientfuturebiblestudy. You can also connect to the series and its author on Facebook.

Introduction to *Abraham: Father of All Believers*

Over half of all the people on earth today look to one man as the pioneer of their relationship with God. Twelve million Jews, two billion Christians, and one billion Muslims trace the foundation of their belief to the encounter of Abraham with God almost four millennia ago. Though the world more often thinks of these three peoples in terms of a clash of civilizations, divided by hatred and a history of violence and war, the root of each of these global religions is the faith of Abraham. From him and his descendants God wishes to bring only blessings to all the families of the earth.

Abraham is truly the father of the world's monotheists. For most Jews and many Arab Christians and Muslims, that fatherhood is rooted in their DNA. But for most of the world's believers, Abraham's fatherhood has nothing at all to do with blood. All of these religions define "father" more expansively: as the one who gives his children a spiritual outlook, the one who hands on to his children what he has discovered about God. The one who teaches the essential truths of life, the one who transmits tradition and identity to the next generation, is father to his spiritual descendants. For the same reason that male spiritual directors, priests, and rabbis are called father by those they teach and guide, Abraham is father to us all.

Questions to Consider

‡ Why are the descendants of Abraham today embroiled in bitter rivalry rather than enjoying the blessings of living as God's family?

‡ Who are the people I would define as my fathers—biologically, ethnically, and spiritually?

The Uncontrollable God of Abraham

Only a small percentage of all the stories told about Abraham in the traditions of Judaism, Christianity, and Islam are found in the Bible. A scholar of the twelfth century, Maimonides, compiled a great summary of Jewish belief in the *Mishneh Torah*. In that work, he offered a narrative of Abraham's youthful career, collected from the stories handed down by the rabbis through the ages. He described the Mesopotamian culture into which Abraham was born as a society utterly lacking awareness of truth and worshiping an array of gods. Terah, the father of Abram (the name of Abraham before his covenant with God), made and sold idols of these gods in his shop. When he put his son in charge of his shop, Abram ridiculed the buyers for bowing down to these objects fresh out of the kiln.

One day a pious woman came to the shop to present a grain offering to the idols. Feeling mischievous, young Abram took a hammer and smashed his father's entire stock, except for the largest statue. He put the hammer into its hand and awaited his father's return. Terah was stunned by the destruction and demanded to know who had rampaged his store. Abram explained that the woman had set the grain before the idols and each one had demanded to eat first, resulting in a bitter fight in which the largest idol took the hammer and smashed all the others. Terah was, of course, incredulous, shouting that he couldn't be fooled. "These idols don't know anything," he said. Abram replied, "Do your ears not hear what your mouth has just said?" Terah was apparently left speechless.

The tradition describes the young Abram as a thoughtful man whose speculative mind gradually came to a preliminary understanding of God. Inspired by the transcendent unity of creation, Abram reasoned that the world was not the work of a committee of gods but of one magnificent Artist. This one God, who later revealed himself to Abram and whom Abraham came to know as El Shaddai and El Olam, is also the YHWH of Israel, the Abba of Jesus, and the Allah of Muhammad. The God of Abraham, Isaac, and Jacob is the creating and redeeming God of us all.

The God who revealed himself first to Abraham, and gradually through Abraham's descendants, can never be fully known. What we know of God from the Bible is only a glimpse of his awesome majesty and profound depths. The One who called Abraham to leave his homeland and wander about the land of Canaan in tents is a God who refuses to be stationary or restrained. The three religious traditions that stem from Abraham all teach that it is utterly impossible to define God fully or to confine God completely in any image, temple, or institution made with human hands.

Questions to Consider

‡ Why are there so many names for the one God in the Bible? Why has God only gradually revealed his identity and true nature to the peoples of the earth?

‡ What are the ways in which people through the ages have attempted to define or confine God? Why is this ultimately impossible?

Founding Father of Judaism, Christianity, and Islam

The people of Israel trace their lineage back to Abraham. If their exodus from Egypt was the birth canal through which they passed to their freedom, and their encounter with God on Mount Sinai the moment of their birth, their conception was the covenant God made with Abraham. When God passed through the separated parts of Abraham's sacrifice with his fiery torch (Gen. 15), he conceived a new people who would develop through the stages of gestation for four hundred years, through Isaac, Jacob, and their children, down to the call of Moses. All Jews look to Abraham as both the biological and the spiritual beginning of their life as a people. They trace their lineage through Abraham's son Isaac, his son Jacob, and Jacob's twelve sons, who were the founders of Israel's twelve tribes.

The Gospels of the New Testament underscore that Jesus is a son of Abraham. Tracing his lineage through King David and back to Abraham, the evangelists accentuate the Judaism of Jesus and his messianic roots. As Israel's Messiah, Jesus brought the history of Abraham's descendants to a peak. Yet his saving mission was not limited in scope to only the children of Israel. The universal dimension of God's plan begun in Abraham, a plan to bring blessings to all the nations, began to be realized in Jesus and was spread through the evangelizing mission of his disciples. For the world's Christians, Abraham is their spiritual father, the one in whom God's history of salvation began. By belonging to Christ, Christians see themselves as Abraham's offspring, a multitude as uncountable as the stars of the sky. For Christians, a family tree is less important than faith; blood is less important than belief.

In the Qur'an of Islam, Abraham (*Ibrahim*, in Arabic) is the primary example of what it means to be a Muslim, "one who submits to God." He is viewed as the true founder of Islam, and Muslims invoke him daily in prayer. The accounts of Abraham's offspring begin with a conflict between two women, one from Mesopotamia, his beloved wife Sarah, the other from Egypt, Sarah's servant Hagar. Abraham's first child, Ishmael, is born from Hagar; later Isaac is born from Sarah. The biblical stories of the two sons are strikingly balanced. Though Ishmael is expelled from Abraham's house at the insistence of Sarah, he is not excluded from Abraham's affection and paternity. Though Isaac receives the inheritance of Abraham, Ishmael is also abundantly blessed by God. There is no victor and loser here. Ishmael later marries an Egyptian and fathers twelve tribes and becomes the leader of a great nation. According to both Jewish and Islamic tradition, this great nation descended from Ishmael is the Arab people.

The Bible and the most essential traditions of Judaism, Christianity, and Islam demonstrate that the God of Abraham is not the possession of any single race or people. Abraham lived before the historical expressions of each of these religions and is looked upon by all as their founding ancestor. Today the truth that Abraham discovered about God is dispersed to every corner of the world. When the descendants of Abraham look back to their origin, they discover that they are all offspring of the same father, members of the same family. The carefully balanced message of the stories of Abraham is that God cares for all of his children.

Could not, then, the father of all believers be a source of healing and reconciliation for the divided children of God? What if religion began to be seen as a source of unity and a bearer of peace rather than a force for division and strife among people? What if Abraham could save the world from the cultural clash between the East and the West that defines the violent world of the twenty-first century? What if we could truly realize what the ancient Scriptures proclaim about Abraham: "Through him, all the nations of the earth shall be blessed."

Questions to Consider

‡ In what way is Abraham the founding father of each of the three major monotheistic religions?

‡ In what way is the crisis in the Middle East a sibling rivalry? What could end the fighting and begin the reconciliation?

The Holy Places of Abraham

The monotheistic religions most often associate three sacred places with Abraham: the Kaaba is Islam's most sanctified shrine in the center of the great mosque at Mecca; the Foundation Stone is the top of the bedrock in Jerusalem around which is built the Dome of the Rock; and the Machpelah is the burial cave of Abraham in Hebron. Unfortunately, these three sites are some of the most tense and well-guarded places on earth.

Every year, during the annual *hajj* (pilgrimage), millions of Muslims from around the world travel to Mecca in Saudi Arabia. The Kaaba (cube, in Arabic), the sacred building in the center of the great mosque, is their primary goal. Every day, followers of Muhammad throughout the world turn in prayer to face this sacred site. The Kaaba, which is about thirty-five feet by forty feet wide and fifty feet tall, is called the house of Allah. The Qur'an says that Abraham found the primordial temple on one of his visits to Arabia to visit his son Ishmael and Ishmael's mother, Hagar. Muslims believe that Abraham reconstructed the Kaaba at its present site with the assistance of Ishmael, building it precisely, stone by stone, in perfect submission to God's commands.

After Abraham completed the restoration of the Kaaba, God commanded him to go to the top of a nearby hill and summon all of humanity to make a pilgrimage to the site. God amplified Abraham's voice so that it could be heard around the world. The pilgrimage became one of the five pillars of Islam, and every Muslim who is physically and financially able is required to go to Mecca on pilgrimage at least once in a lifetime. When pilgrims enter the Grand Mosque, after purifying themselves and donning white garments, they circle the Kaaba seven times, praying in unity with Abraham. In other events during the weeklong festivities, pilgrims run between the hills of the nearby Safa and Marwa, remembering Hagar's frantic search for water for Ishmael as her son was dying in the wilderness. Pilgrims also throw seven pebbles at a stone pillar that represents the devil, who tried to tempt Abraham to ignore God's command to sacrifice his son (in Muslim tradition, the son is Ishmael, not Isaac). The pilgrims then sacrifice a sheep, reenacting the story of Abraham sacrificing the ram that God provided as a substitute.

The most prominent structure in the city of Jerusalem is the golden Dome of the Rock. This beautiful Islamic shrine from the seventh century was built over the large outcropping of bedrock on the site where Solomon's temple once stood. Biographers of Muhammad describe the mystical night journey in which the prophet came to this spot to join Jesus and earlier prophets for prayer. Here, at this holy place, which people had believed for centuries to be a connecting point between heaven and earth, Muhammad briefly ascended into heaven to meet God, then returned to earth.

Jewish tradition has always considered this place as the site of Mount Moriah, where Abraham bound Isaac for sacrifice. On the feast of New Year, Rosh Hashanah, Jews blow the ram's horn (*shofar*) during synagogue services to commemorate the Akedah, the binding of Isaac. The blowing of the horn, while calling to mind the faith of Abraham, which led him to offer his son to God, is meant to arouse God's compassion. Through the merits of Abraham, God forgives the sins of men and women as he judges them on Rosh Hashanah.

Mount Moriah and Mount Zion are one and the same. After King David conquered Jerusalem, he purchased this site for the future temple. For centuries, the smoke of animal sacrifice ascended from the temple to God, as God's people continued to offer daily the substitute offering that God provided in lieu of Abraham's son. In Christian tradition, the sacrifices at the temple are a foreshadowing of the climactic work of Christ, offered in sacrifice by the Father for the sins of the whole world. The binding of Isaac, the crucifixion, and the *dhabih* (the Qur'an's version of Abraham's offering) are events at the heart of the self-understanding of Judaism, Christianity, and Islam. The fact that all three religions recount the excruciating suffering of a father preparing for the death of his son, the most unimaginable kind of anguish, points to the shared origins and the core of obedient divine love at the foundation of these three Abrahamic faiths.

From the temple mount of Jerusalem, the sounds of the three great religions can be heard in the distance: the blowing of the shofar, the ringing of church bells, and the Muslim prayers amplified from the minarets. People today take for granted this dissonance of sounds. For many people of the world, these are the sounds that represent a bitter history of antagonism and conflicting worldviews. But if we look to Abraham, and if we look to the truest teachings of the founders who followed him—Moses, Jesus, and Muhammad—these three sounds could become a harmonious triad of peace for all the world to hear.

Finally, the cave of Machpelah in Hebron is the burial place of Abraham. In Arabic it is called *Haram el-Khalil*, "the sacred precinct of the friend of God." Originally the patriarch purchased this cave for the final resting place of his wife Sarah. After the death of Abraham, he was buried here also, as were his descendants Isaac and Jacob, along with their wives, Rebekah and Leah. Today this site is heavily guarded and hotly disputed by Israeli Jews and Palestinian Arabs, the scene of much bloodshed throughout the centuries and into most recent times. Serving as a synagogue, a church, and a mosque at different times in history, this resting place of Abraham is the second most uneasy site in the Holy Land, next to the temple mount.

Yet, when Abraham died (as Genesis records in one of the most hopeful passages of the Hebrew Scriptures), his two sons, Ishmael and Isaac, who had been rivals since their births, stood side by side to bury their father in the cave of Machpelah. Ishmael, the patriarch of the Muslim people, and Isaac, the patriarch of Jews and the spiritual ancestor of Christians, shared their pain that day and recognized that they were brothers, children of the same father. Could not this scene of painful reconciliation be a symbol for new understanding and sympathetic dialogue among the world's three great monotheistic religions? Could not the shared grief that gives birth to forgiveness be the spark that sets the world alight with new hope for peace in the twenty-first century?

Questions to Consider

‡ What is the spiritual value in pilgrimage to sacred places?

‡ How could the cave of Machpelah in Hebron be a symbol of reconciliation for the clashing descendants of Abraham?

Ancestor of Us All

Read this inspired text, listening for its fuller meaning in light of the whole plan of God.

ROMANS 4:11–12

¹¹[Abraham] received the sign of circumcision as a seal of the righteousness that he had by faith while he was still uncircumcised. The purpose was to make him the ancestor of all who believe with-

out being circumcised and who thus have righteousness reckoned to them, [12]and likewise the ancestor of the circumcised who are not only circumcised but who also follow the example of the faith that our ancestor Abraham had before he was circumcised.

Continue exploring the meaning of Paul's words through the tradition of the church.

In writing to the Christians in Rome, Paul demonstrates that Abraham is "the ancestor of all who believe" (v. 11). For the early church, this meant that both Jewish and Gentile followers of Jesus, the circumcised and the uncircumcised, could enter a saving relationship with God and thus claim Abraham as their father. Neither is pitted against the other. All people can become descendants of Abraham by sharing his faith.

In the life of Abraham, as Paul demonstrates, faith was the priority. Abraham was made righteous before God through his faithful trust. His circumcision was a subsequent seal of his righteousness, not the producer of his saving relationship with God. Thus Abraham is the bearer of God's promised blessings to all people, not just the Jewish people. All who believe in the God of Abraham are Abraham's children.

Meditatio

Consider the meaning of this Scripture passage in the context of your own life in Christ today.

✝ In what ways do people sometimes erect unnecessary barriers that divide people rather than unify them?

✝ How can faith in the God of Abraham be a means of dialogue and understanding among Jews, Christians, and Muslims?

Oratio

Respond in prayer with the hope that arises within you.

God of Abraham, Sarah, and Hagar, you have promised blessings to all the peoples of the earth. Open my heart to a spirit of forgiveness toward those who share my life, and help me be a minister of reconciliation to struggling and broken people. May the peace you desire for the world begin through an understanding of the inspired texts of our ancestors in faith. Enlighten and encourage me as I read and contemplate your inspired Word in these sacred Scriptures. Show me how to make my life a testimony to God's love.

Continue to pray to God from your heart . . .

Contemplatio

Remain in quiet and place yourself under God's loving gaze. Ask God to give you an experience of shalom (Hebrew), salaam (Arabic), peace.

Operatio

How can I best dedicate myself to the reflective study of these sacred texts of Abraham over the coming weeks? What regular place and time could I choose for the quiet practice of lectio divina?

1

Abram Goes Forth at the Call of God

Lectio

Close off the distractions around you and enter a moment of stillness.
Breathe in, being filled with the presence of God's Spirit. Breathe out, letting
go of all that could distract you from this sacred time.

GENESIS 12:1–9

¹Now the LORD said to Abram, "Go from your country and your kindred and your father's house to the land that I will show you. ²I will make of you a great nation, and I will bless you, and make your name great, so that you will be a blessing. ³I will bless those who bless you, and the one who curses you I will curse; and in you all the families of the earth shall be blessed."

⁴So Abram went, as the LORD had told him; and Lot went with him. Abram was seventy-five years old when he departed from Haran. ⁵Abram took his wife Sarai and his brother's son Lot, and all the possessions that they had gathered, and the persons whom they had acquired in Haran; and they set forth to go to the land of Canaan. When they had come to the land of Canaan, ⁶Abram passed through the land to the place at Shechem, to the oak of Moreh. At that time the Canaanites were in the land. ⁷Then the LORD appeared to Abram,

and said, "To your offspring I will give this land." So he built there an altar to the Lord, who had appeared to him. ⁸From there he moved on to the hill country on the east of Bethel, and pitched his tent, with Bethel on the west and Ai on the east; and there he built an altar to the Lord and invoked the name of the Lord. ⁹And Abram journeyed on by stages toward the Negeb.

After allowing the Scripture to penetrate your mind and heart, listen for further understanding through this commentary.

Abram had already lived much of his life. He no longer possessed the vigor of youth or the gullibility and hearty desire for fortune and fame that often characterizes young adulthood. He had earned a secure life in his Mesopotamian culture. But in the middle of life, after his father had died, Abram received the call to begin again.

God's word to Abram, "Go" (v. 1), presents an imperative and an invitation. The enormity of what God asks and of the decision to be made is expressed through the threefold listing of what Abram must leave: "your country and your kindred and your father's house." The terms are arranged in ascending order according to the severity of the sacrifice involved: the region of Mesopotamia, his ethnic group, and his extended family. God's call demanded that he leave the basis of his security, trade, and identity. He must transfer his orientation from his homeland and his lineage to God and God's promises.

At the center of Abram's call are the wondrous promises of God. These promises are the key to the entire Bible and will be fulfilled throughout the history of salvation. The initial set of promises expresses God's commitment to Abram: first, to make of him a great nation; second, to bless him with abundant flocks, numerous offspring, good health, and long life; and third, to make his name great so that he will be esteemed with a noble reputation (v. 2). The second set of promises shows how God will affect other nations through Abram and how God will protect Abram among the nations (v. 3). Most amazingly, God proclaims the highest goal of Abram's calling: "In you all the families of the earth shall be blessed" (v. 3). Through Abram and his descendants, God will bestow universal blessings to all the people of the world.

In unwavering obedience to the divine call, Abram accepts his new identity: "Abram went" (v. 4). At age seventy-five, Abram has the vision to see beyond his own lifetime and the wisdom to understand the importance of making sacrifices for future generations. Every aging person wants to leave a legacy, and Abram's legacy would extend farther than anyone could imagine.

The journey of Abram from the homeland of his ancestors, Ur, to Haran, and then, at the call of God, to Shechem in the land of Canaan, took him along some of the most ancient roads and through some of the most important cities and lands of the ancient world. Archaeology has revealed that Shechem (v. 6) and Bethel (v. 8) were already Canaanite religious shrines before Abram arrived. Abram built altars there and worshipped God. Here God gave Abram another promise: "To your offspring I will give this land" (v. 7). Hereafter, the history of Abram's descendents is inextricably bound to the Promised Land. Continuing southward, he reached the Negeb, having traversed the entire length of the land, marking out the land of promise.

Abram was a spiritual pioneer. He took the necessary risk and made the inevitable sacrifices for a future he would never see. His every action, then, gained a significance that transcended his own lifetime and would eventually change the whole world.

After listening to this passage, read the commentary carefully and write your answers to these questions:

✝ Which words stand out to you when you read the call of Abram aloud?

✝ What was Abram required to leave behind when he heard the call of God to "go" forth (v. 1)?

Meditatio

Ask yourself what God is saying to you through this text of Scripture. Allow the call of Abram to interact with your own experiences of fear and hope.

‡ Abram received a divine call in the middle of his life to begin again. When have I overcome the fear of change in order to make a new beginning?

‡ Abram's decision in his advancing years changed the world for all his descendants. What is the legacy I want to leave beyond my own lifetime?

‡ In what way is Abram a model for me of trust in the future? What can I do to demonstrate a greater trust in the future God has in store for me?

Oratio

Use these or similar words to respond to God, who speaks to you through the Scriptures.

> Lord God, you called Abram to leave his familiar homeland in order to begin again. Help me trust in your promises to me and overcome the fear of change. Give me the grace to make a fresh start and the wisdom to hope in the future.

Continue to pray to God from your heart . . .

Contemplatio

For a few quiet moments, rest with confidence in the promises God has given to you. Let your trust in God's promises reach into your heart and dispel your fear.

After a period of silent contemplation, write a few words about your experience.

Operatio

The inspired Scriptures have the power to change us from within. What can I do today to begin to live out the future God has promised me? In what way have these verses made me more hopeful?

2

Abram and Sarai in Egypt

Lectio

As you read the Scripture and commentary, highlight or underline passages that seem most pertinent to you. These marks will help you recall your experience of hearing the Scripture and seeking to understand its significance.

GENESIS 12:10–20

[10]Now there was a famine in the land. So Abram went down to Egypt to reside there as an alien, for the famine was severe in the land. [11]When he was about to enter Egypt, he said to his wife Sarai, "I know well that you are a woman beautiful in appearance; [12]and when the Egyptians see you, they will say, 'This is his wife'; then they will kill me, but they will let you live. [13]Say you are my sister, so that it may go well with me because of you, and that my life may be spared on your account." [14]When Abram entered Egypt the Egyptians saw that the woman was very beautiful. [15]When the officials of Pharaoh saw her, they praised her to Pharaoh. And the woman was taken into Pharaoh's house. [16]And for her sake he dealt well with Abram; and he had sheep, oxen, male donkeys, male and female slaves, female donkeys, and camels.

[17]But the LORD afflicted Pharaoh and his house with great plagues because of Sarai, Abram's wife. [18]So Pharaoh called Abram, and said, "What is this you have done to me? Why did you not tell me that she

was your wife? ¹⁹Why did you say, 'She is my sister,' so that I took her for my wife? Now then, here is your wife, take her, and be gone." ²⁰And Pharaoh gave his men orders concerning him; and they set him on the way, with his wife and all that he had.

After listening to the words of this text and imagining the scene, continue to explore their significance through these remarks.

The Bible consistently shows the heroes of faith as they really are, not as we might wish them to be. This account of Abram stands in sharp contrast to the trusting faith demonstrated by his response to God's call. Here the patriarch is shown in all of his human frailty, threatened by famine and physical peril and seeking desperate solutions. When people are put in extreme circumstances, they often face excruciating choices about how to survive.

The "famine in the land" (v. 10) indicates that living in the Promised Land was harsh and often precarious. Though famine could result from any number of natural or human causes, the most common cause in Canaan was the failure of the seasonal rains. In contrast to Canaan, Egypt could depend on the more predictable rise of the Nile River for its rich fertility. So Abram and his wife Sarai went to live in Egypt in order to survive the famine.

Because of Sarai's surpassing beauty, Abram feared that some Egyptian might murder him in order to take her. So Abram asked Sarai to pass herself off as his sister, which she agreed to do (vv. 11–13). Jewish and Christian commentaries on this story judge Abram's conduct in a variety of ways. Some condemn Abram's choice for placing his virtuous wife in a compromising situation because of his own fear of being killed. Others describe his dilemma as a choice between two evils. If Abram told the truth, he would surely be killed and Sarai would be condemned to abuse and shame. His deception at least assured the survival of both of them.

Another judgment on this account is based on the ancient norm that, in the absence of a father, the brother assumed legal guardianship of his sister with responsibilities for arranging her marriage. Perhaps Abram reasoned that, by posing as Sarai's brother, he could force whoever wanted to take

Sarai as a wife to negotiate with him. This would buy some time until the famine lifted, allowing both of them to escape and return to Canaan.

As expected, Sarai's extraordinary beauty attracted the attention of Pharaoh's officials, and she was brought into the harem of Pharaoh. In turn, Pharaoh bestowed abundant gifts on Abram in return for Sarai (vv. 15–16). The helpless couple is faced with the overwhelming power of imperial Egypt. Abram is saved, but Sarai is trapped in a seemingly hopeless situation that threatens the promises God has made.

In the end, God intervenes to rescue those he has chosen (v. 17). The nature of the plague is not described, but the literature of Jewish midrash delights in describing the severe genital inflammation that must have afflicted Pharaoh as his passion for Sarai was stirred. Pharaoh is infuriated at Abram for his trickery and orders his men to escort Abram and Sarai, with all their possessions, out of the country (vv. 18–20).

Many ancient epics recount a story of the abduction of the hero's beautiful wife. In most of these, a military campaign (even to the scope of the Trojan War) is launched to recover her. But in the epic of Abraham, God is the deliverer. The story shows the length to which God will go, when all human resources have failed, to deliver his chosen ones and to protect the promises he has made to them.

The experiences of Abram and Sarai prefigure the experience of their offspring many generations later in the exodus. Like their ancestors, the descendants of Abram and Sarai would journey to Egypt to escape a famine in Canaan. Later, their welcome would fade and Pharaoh would subject them to his own will. In order to rescue the descendants of Abram and Sarai from bondage, God would inflict plagues upon Pharaoh, convincing Pharaoh to eject the Israelites. Escaping from Egypt ahead of Pharaoh's army, Israel would take with them all the goods they had received from the Egyptians.

After marking the Scripture and commentary, write out your answer to this question:

‡ Which of the explanations offered seems the most probable reason for Abram's desire to pass off Sarai as his sister?

Meditatio

After reflecting on the text you have read, spend some time thinking about its implications for your life. Write out your answers to these questions:

‡ Why do I think the biblical authors chose to highlight the human weaknesses and shortcomings of biblical heroes? How is this helpful to me in seeking to learn from their experiences with God?

‡ When have I made a difficult choice in an extreme circumstance? In what way did God deliver me or come to my rescue?

‡ Does Abram's trick indicate a lack of trust in God? In what way is trust an essential ingredient of marriage or friendship?

Oratio

Speak to God using the words of this prayer or those of your own.

> God of love, through enduring sacrifices and sharing goals, Abram
> and Sarai became models of devotion. Help me to trust in you in the
> midst of life's adversities, and help me to imitate the dedication of
> my ancestors.

Articulate your feelings to the One who accepts you completely ...

Contemplatio

*Spend some moments in quiet, simply placing yourself under the loving care
of God, who is always with us in times of confusion and doubt. Ask God to
point you in the right direction.*

*After your time of silent contemplation, write a few words about your
experience.*

Operatio

God's Word shapes us and changes us. How might Abram and Sarai have
changed as a result of this experience? How is this Scripture passage helping me to change in relationship to God?

3

The Families of Abram
and Lot Separate

Lectio

*Read this passage aloud so that you may simultaneously read with your eyes
and listen with your ears.*

GENESIS 13:1–18

¹So Abram went up from Egypt, he and his wife, and all that he had,
and Lot with him, into the Negeb. ²Now Abram was very rich in livestock, in silver, and in gold. ³He journeyed on by stages from the Negeb
as far as Bethel, to the place where his tent had been at the beginning,
between Bethel and Ai, ⁴to the place where he had made an altar at the
first; and there Abram called on the name of the LORD. ⁵Now Lot, who
went with Abram, also had flocks and herds and tents, ⁶so that the land
could not support both of them living together; for their possessions were
so great that they could not live together, ⁷and there was strife between
the herders of Abram's livestock and the herders of Lot's livestock. At
that time the Canaanites and the Perizzites lived in the land.

⁸Then Abram said to Lot, "Let there be no strife between you and
me, and between your herders and my herders; for we are kindred. ⁹Is
not the whole land before you? Separate yourself from me. If you take

the left hand, then I will go to the right; or if you take the right hand, then I will go to the left." [10]Lot looked about him, and saw that the plain of the Jordan was well watered everywhere like the garden of the LORD, like the land of Egypt, in the direction of Zoar; this was before the LORD had destroyed Sodom and Gomorrah. [11]So Lot chose for himself all the plain of the Jordan, and Lot journeyed eastward; thus they separated from each other. [12]Abram settled in the land of Canaan, while Lot settled among the cities of the Plain and moved his tent as far as Sodom. [13]Now the people of Sodom were wicked, great sinners against the LORD.

[14]The LORD said to Abram, after Lot had separated from him, "Raise your eyes now, and look from the place where you are, northward and southward and eastward and westward; [15]for all the land that you see I will give to you and to your offspring forever. [16]I will make your offspring like the dust of the earth; so that if one can count the dust of the earth, your offspring also can be counted. [17]Rise up, walk through the length and the breadth of the land, for I will give it to you." [18]So Abram moved his tent, and came and settled by the oaks of Mamre, which are at Hebron; and there he built an altar to the LORD.

Continue to search for the meaning and significance of this passage through this commentary.

Lot, the nephew of Abram, had journeyed with Abram and Sarai from Haran and now has traveled with the couple from Egypt back into the Promised Land (v. 1). It was customary that the oldest uncle should assume the guardianship of the child of his deceased brother. The childless Abram must have grown to love his nephew Lot as if he were his own son. Yet, there comes a time when adults must separate from their grown children and surrender them to the world outside their family. Though Abram and Sarai had deeply invested their time and love in Lot, it was now time to let go and let Lot find his own way.

In a nomadic culture in which herders were dependent on available grazing land and watering places, environmental realities placed a limit on the size of herds and encampments. With friction growing between the herders of Abram's livestock and those of Lot over available pasturage and water, Abram decides to take action (vv. 5–7). Showing nobility of character, Abram selflessly offers his nephew first choice of grazing land. Though one would expect Lot to defer to his uncle, Lot quickly chooses the more attractive land of the Jordan Plain (vv. 8–11).

Lot's greed eventually turns out to be his downfall. Dazzled by the appearance of abundance, Lot imagines prosperity in the fertile valley and is attracted to the stimuli of the cities of the Plain (vv. 12–13). Abram, on the other hand, inherits the more rugged hills of Canaan, an area where dependence on God seems more necessary, a place where trust and peace can be cultivated.

After Lot has departed, God firmly links Abram's future to the land. At God's invitation, Abram looks north toward Shechem, south toward Hebron, east toward the Jordan River, and west toward the Mediterranean. God assures Abram that this will be the land of his offspring forever (vv. 14–15). His descendants, God says, will be like the dust of the earth— beyond numbering (v. 16). Finally, Abram is told to walk the length and breadth of the land (v. 17), a symbolic action indicating that the land will belong to Abram and he will belong to the land. He settles near the trees of Mamre, in the vicinity of Hebron. These great oaks served as a landmark as well as welcome shade in the hot and windy climate.

After listening to this passage, see if you can answer the following questions:

✝ Why was it necessary that Abram and Lot separate from one another?

✝ What are the spiritual advantages of settling in the rugged hills of Canaan rather than the fertile plains?

Meditatio

While reflecting on this passage, consider the connections between the life of Abram and your own life today.

✝ How did Abram know it was time to separate from Lot? How do parents and adult children know when it is time to let go and separate from one another?

✝ In what ways does God link Abram's future to the land? Why is God's promise of land so important for Abram?

✝ What is the land God has given me? To what places is my identity particularly bound? How does the locale in which I live help me cultivate a life for God?

Oratio

Pray to God in these words or in the words that issue from your own heart.

Lord God, when I look to the north, south, east, and west, I realize that I am surrounded by reminders of your presence. I want to cultivate a life that gives honor to you. Help me to treasure your gifts that surround me and to use them for your greater glory.

Express your gratitude to God for the many reminders of his goodness around you . . .

Contemplatio

Rest in God's presence, knowing that God provides for all that you need. Repeat the word "trust" to keep you focused and aware of God.

After your time of silence, write a brief note about your experience of contemplation.

Operatio

The Scriptures have the power to change our attitudes from within. How can I better express my gratitude today to God and to those dear to me?

4

Abram Blessed by Melchizedek

Lectio

*Create a sacred space around you and sanctify this time of lectio by lighting
a candle, ringing a chime, or kissing the page of Scripture as you begin to
read. Read this Scripture aloud, listening to the words with your ears as you
speak them with your voice.*

GENESIS 14:17–24

[17]After his [Abraham's] return from the defeat of Chedorlaomer
and the kings who were with him, the king of Sodom went out to
meet him at the Valley of Shaveh (that is, the King's Valley). [18]And
King Melchizedek of Salem brought out bread and wine; he was
priest of God Most High. [19]He blessed him and said,

> "Blessed be Abram by God Most High,
> maker of heaven and earth;
> [20]and blessed be God Most High,
> who has delivered your enemies into your hand!"

And Abram gave him one tenth of everything.
[21]Then the king of Sodom said to Abram, "Give me the persons, but
take the goods for yourself." [22]But Abram said to the king of Sodom,

"I have sworn to the LORD, God Most High, maker of heaven and earth, [23]that I would not take a thread or a sandal-thong or anything that is yours, so that you might not say, 'I have made Abram rich.' [24]I will take nothing but what the young men have eaten, and the share of the men who went with me—Aner, Eshcol, and Mamre. Let them take their share.'"

After listening for God's Word in this inspired text, keep listening for greater understanding through the teachings and scholarship of the church.

Genesis 14 describes a surprising new feature of Abram's personality: the courageous warrior-chieftain. A confederacy of four kings from the East had subjugated the city-states of the area around the Dead Sea for many years and had returned to suppress a rebellion. While plundering Sodom and surrounding cities, the kings' forces took large amounts of booty and some captives, including Abram's nephew Lot (vv. 1–12).

On learning the news of Lot's capture, Abram again demonstrates his self-sacrificing loyalty to his family in time of need. Abram mustered a force of 318 men and mounted an armed campaign to rescue his nephew. Taking advantage of darkness and surprising his foes, Abram routed the enemies. They fled so quickly that they left all the spoils, along with Lot and other captives (vv. 13–16).

As Abram was returning home triumphantly, he was met by two monarchs: the king of Sodom and the king of Salem. The kings came out from their cities to meet the patriarch, whose victory had benefited the entire region. The contrast between these two kings could not be greater. The king of Sodom, whose name is not mentioned, came out to meet his benefactor empty-handed, and the first word he uttered was "Give" (v. 21) The king of Salem, whose name is Melchizedek, brought out bread and wine for a victory feast with Abram and his men, and he offered a blessing for Abram.

Melchizedek is both a king and a priest, and as such he invoked a blessing on Abram (vv. 18–19). Hebrew tradition identified Salem with Jerusalem (Ps. 76:2), and the place where the king and patriarch met, the King's Valley (v. 17), is right outside the walls of Jerusalem. The divine name and title evoked by Melchizedek, "God Most High, maker of heaven and earth," is also the name by which Abram called upon God (vv. 19–20, 22). The writer of Genesis is making the bold claim that the one God who called Abram was indistinctly known in the chief god of the Canaanite pantheon. Truly the God of Abraham is the universal God who will bless all peoples of the earth. In denying any claim to the spoils he had won in war, Abram shows that his trust in God was complete (vv. 22–23). He would depend on no earthly king for his wealth but in the maker of heaven and earth.

Melchizedek is mentioned only one other time in the Hebrew Scriptures. In a royal psalm extolling the Davidic ruler of Jerusalem, it is said of the king, "You are a priest forever according to the order of Melchizedek" (Ps. 110:4). Like Melchizedek, the Canaanite predecessor of the Davidic king in the pre-Israelite Jerusalem, the Israelite king was both priest and king, chief mediator between God and people. Melchizedek's service as priest to Abram immortalized him as the model of sacred kingship and of a priestly messiah. The writer of the book of Hebrews interprets the ministry of Jesus as the fulfillment of Melchizedek's line (see Heb. 7:1–22).

After reading the Scripture and commentary, write out your answers to these questions:

☦ What are the primary characteristics of the king of Salem?

☦ In what way is the future Messiah of Israel like Melchizedek?

Meditatio

Spend some time reflecting on the meaning of the Scripture passage for your own life. After meditating on each question, write out your answer to each.

‡ Abram was loyal to his nephew despite Lot's less-than-honorable treatment of his uncle. How do I respond when a member of my family is in trouble? What does the example of Abram teach me about family loyalty?

‡ In what way did Abram's acknowledgment of God as "maker of heaven and earth" enable him to trust? How does my understanding of God help me to trust?

‡ How does my understanding that Israel's Messiah is both king and priest help me to think about Jesus Christ? How do I honor him as king and priest?

Oratio

Pray to God from your heart using these words and then continue with words of your own.

Most High God, you are the creator of heaven and earth. Bind my family to you and help me to be loyal to the people you have given to me as my family. Show me how to live with trusting confidence in you and to know that you provide all that I need.

Ask God from your heart for the gift of confidence...

Contemplatio

Letting go of all need for words or reason, spend some still moments trying to experience God's protective power surrounding you.

After your time of silence, spend a moment writing a few notes about your experience of contemplation.

Operatio

In what way can I be a more consistent provider and protector for those I love? What can I do this week to help them trust me more?

5

God Seals the Covenant
with Abram

Lectio

Ask the Holy Spirit to guide your reading so that you grow to understand the
message and inspired truth God wishes you to understand from this text.
Before you begin reading, close your eyes and imagine the night sky full of
stars. As you read the biblical verses, listen for God's voice within the words of
the inspired text.

GENESIS 15:1–21

¹After these things the word of the LORD came to Abram in a vision,
"Do not be afraid, Abram, I am your shield; your reward shall be very
great." ²But Abram said, "O LORD God, what will you give me, for I
continue childless, and the heir of my house is Eliezer of Damascus?"
³And Abram said, "You have given me no offspring, and so a slave
born in my house is to be my heir." ⁴But the word of the LORD came
to him, "This man shall not be your heir; no one but your very own
issue shall be your heir." ⁵He brought him outside and said, "Look
toward heaven and count the stars, if you are able to count them."
Then he said to him, "So shall your descendants be." ⁶And he believed
the LORD; and the LORD reckoned it to him as righteousness.

⁷Then he said to him, "I am the LORD who brought you from Ur of the Chaldeans, to give you this land to possess." ⁸But he said, "O LORD God, how am I to know that I shall possess it?" ⁹He said to him, "Bring me a heifer three years old, a female goat three years old, a ram three years old, a turtledove, and a young pigeon." ¹⁰He brought him all these and cut them in two, laying each half over against the other; but he did not cut the birds in two. ¹¹And when birds of prey came down on the carcasses, Abram drove them away.

¹²As the sun was going down, a deep sleep fell upon Abram, and a deep and terrifying darkness descended upon him. ¹³Then the LORD said to Abram, "Know this for certain, that your offspring shall be aliens in a land that is not theirs, and shall be slaves there, and they shall be oppressed for four hundred years; ¹⁴but I will bring judgment on the nation that they serve, and afterward they shall come out with great possessions. ¹⁵As for yourself, you shall go to your ancestors in peace; you shall be buried in a good old age. ¹⁶And they shall come back here in the fourth generation; for the iniquity of the Amorites is not yet complete."

¹⁷When the sun had gone down and it was dark, a smoking fire pot and a flaming torch passed between these pieces. ¹⁸On that day the LORD made a covenant with Abram, saying, "To your descendants I give this land, from the river of Egypt to the great river, the river Euphrates, ¹⁹the land of the Kenites, the Kenizzites, the Kadmonites, ²⁰the Hittites, the Perizzites, the Rephaim, ²¹the Amorites, the Canaanites, the Girgashites, and the Jebusites."

Continue searching for the significance of this text through the tradition of God's people.

"Do not be afraid" (v. 1), God calls to Abram. Faith like Abram's does not develop in an instant. It must grow stronger over time as fears are faced and overcome. God wants Abram to believe the promise despite the logical improbabilities of its being fulfilled. The years had been passing by, and the promised heir had not materialized. Again God assures Abram with another intangible promise: "Your reward shall be very great." But Abram's pent-up frustrations had reached their limit. He bursts forth with his doubts and disappointments: "O LORD God, what will you give me, for I continue childless?" (v. 2). No material reward could ever equal the blessing of having a child.

The covenant promises are divided into two sections: verses 1–5 focus on the promise of posterity; verses 7–21 focus on the gift of land. The first promise is made at night in a vision (v. 1, 5); the second takes place at sundown in a "deep sleep" (v. 12). The twin promises are interconnected; one is necessary for the other. God's gifts of descendants and the Promised Land are inseparable.

Abram seems almost resigned to the fallback measure offered to childless couples. According to the ancient custom, the barren couple would adopt a slave to care for them in their old age and assure a proper burial. After their death the adopted servant would become their principal heir (vv. 2–3). Yet, God emphatically assured Abram not only that he would have a child as an heir but also that his offspring would be innumerable (v. 5). To impress on Abram the enormity of this gift, God invited him to contemplate the star-studded night sky: "So shall your descendants be" (v. 5). Abram would have multitudes of offspring by natural birth, complemented by countless children joined to his lineage by faith.

God seals the promise of land by making a covenant with Abram. Covenants were common in the ancient world for defining and sealing various types of relationships. The covenant between God and Abram contained the basic elements of ancient covenants: the identification of the one initiating the covenant, a statement of the history of the two parties entering the covenant, the blessings provided through the relationship (v. 7), and the ceremony of ratifying the covenant (vv. 9–21). In this mysterious ritual of "cutting" the covenant, the animals to be sacrificed are cut in two (v. 10), and the one making the covenant passes between the pieces to solemnly seal the covenant. The ritual expresses the conviction that the parties will suffer the same fate as the animals should they fail to keep the covenant (Jer. 34:18). Here God, represented by the flaming torch, passes between the sundered animals, making a unilateral, unconditional covenant with Abram (v. 17).

The connecting link between God's promises of descendants and land is Abram's faith: "He believed the LORD ; and the LORD reckoned it to him as righteousness" (v. 6). Faith is not defined here; rather the reader is shown what faith is through Abram. He put his full trust in God, even when that trust seemed unwarranted, and thus became the model of faith for us all.

Meditatio

‡ Why do I need to hear God's words, "Do not be afraid" (v. 1)? Why are fears and doubts a necessary part of growing in faith? How has my faith developed through times of fear and doubt?

‡ When have I found it most difficult to trust in God? Am I willing to trust God completely?

‡ What are the promises God has offered to me? In what way does my confidence in God give hope to my life?

Oratio

Pray to God for a gift of faith like that of Abram.

> God my Shield, I believe that you are my protector and the source of all that I need. Help me to look to Abram as my model of faith. Assist me that I might trust completely in you, even when your promises to me seem distant and doubtful.

Ask God to help you trust in him completely...

Contemplatio

Spend some quiet moments resting in God's embrace. Put your life in God's hands and rely on him completely.

After some contemplative moments, write a few words about your experience.

Operatio

How would my life be different if I trusted in God completely? What can I do to begin living that kind of life today?

6

Hagar Gives Birth
to Ishmael

Lectio

Prepare to read the Scripture by asking God's Spirit to open your mind, your lips, and your heart. As you read, consider the emotions in the scene: the frustrated distress of barrenness, nagging contempt and jealousy, the anguish of rejection, and the gloom of desolation.

GENESIS 16:1–16

¹Now Sarai, Abram's wife, bore him no children. She had an Egyptian slave-girl whose name was Hagar, ²and Sarai said to Abram, "You see that the LORD has prevented me from bearing children; go in to my slave-girl; it may be that I shall obtain children by her." And Abram listened to the voice of Sarai. ³So, after Abram had lived ten years in the land of Canaan, Sarai, Abram's wife, took Hagar the Egyptian, her slave-girl, and gave her to her husband Abram as a wife. ⁴He went in to Hagar, and she conceived; and when she saw that she had conceived, she looked with contempt on her mistress. ⁵Then Sarai said to Abram, "May the wrong done to me be on you! I gave my slave-girl to your embrace, and when she saw that she had conceived, she looked on me with contempt. May the LORD judge

between you and me!" ⁶But Abram said to Sarai, "Your slave-girl is in your power; do to her as you please." Then Sarai dealt harshly with her, and she ran away from her.

⁷The angel of the LORD found her by a spring of water in the wilderness, the spring on the way to Shur. ⁸And he said, "Hagar, slave-girl of Sarai, where have you come from and where are you going?" She said, "I am running away from my mistress Sarai." ⁹The angel of the LORD said to her, "Return to your mistress, and submit to her."

¹⁰The angel of the LORD also said to her, "I will so greatly multiply your offspring that they cannot be counted for multitude." ¹¹And the angel of the LORD said to her,

> "Now you have conceived and shall bear a son;
> you shall call him Ishmael,
> for the LORD has given heed to your affliction.
> ¹²He shall be a wild ass of a man,
> with his hand against everyone,
> and everyone's hand against him;
> and he shall live at odds with all his kin."

¹³So she named the LORD who spoke to her, "You are El-roi"; for she said, "Have I really seen God and remained alive after seeing him?" ¹⁴Therefore the well was called Beer-lahai-roi; it lies between Kadesh and Bered. ¹⁵Hagar bore Abram a son; and Abram named his son, whom Hagar bore, Ishmael. ¹⁶Abram was eighty-six years old when Hagar bore him Ishmael.

Continuing with an open mind and heart, search for the meaning of this text through the understanding of the community of faith.

Ten years had elapsed since Abram left Haran with the promise that he would become a great nation (v. 3). The hopes of Abram and Sarai to bear a child reached a critical level of frustration. In desperation, Sarai took the initiative to give Abram an heir and to build their family. She suggested to Abram that he father a child by her Egyptian servant, Hagar (v. 2). The practice of an infertile wife offering a surrogate to her husband was common practice in the ancient Middle East.

Yet, Sarai's well-intended act created a triangle of trouble. The difference between the two women was striking. Sarai was from Abram's tribe, a beautiful but aging woman, free but barren. Hagar was a foreigner, young with the exotic look of an Egyptian, a slave-girl and fertile. Sarai had underestimated her vulnerability to that most unbearable of human emotions: jealousy.

Abram agreed to his wife's plan, and when Abram slept with Hagar, she immediately conceived (v. 4). When Sarai's plan came to fruition, her selflessness deteriorated into angry accusations against her husband and cruelty toward Hagar. We do not know the details of Sarai's harsh treatment of Hagar, but we know it was ruthless enough to cause the pregnant Hagar to flee into the wilderness (v. 6).

Hagar was fleeing in the direction of her homeland when she was met by an angel of God, the first angelic visitation in the biblical literature (v. 7). God's messenger told her to return and submit to her mistress, but he also gave her a series of incredible divine promises. She would have a son, whom she was to name Ishmael. His name means "God hears," for indeed God heard her cry for help and hears the needs of the outcasts. Ishmael's nature was compared to that of the wild ass, a sturdy desert animal whose fierce, fleet-footed love of freedom makes it impossible to domesticate (vv. 11–12). Most amazingly, God said to Hagar, "I will so greatly multiply your offspring that they cannot be counted for multitude" (v. 10). Ishmael himself was destined to become the father of twelve tribes and of a great nation (25:12–18).

Hagar's relationship with God is unique. She is the only person in the Bible to give a name to God: El-roi, the God whom I have seen, the God who sees me (v. 13). Only God, through his messenger, calls Hagar by name—Abram and Sarai had called her only slave-girl. Although Hagar is powerless as female, slave, and foreigner, God hears her, calls her by name, and makes her the mother of a great nation.

Returning to Abram's household, she bore Abram a son. Abram named him Ishmael, designating the boy as his own with all the attendant privileges. For the time being, Abram accepted his son as the fulfillment of God's promise.

Meditatio

Envision this scene in your imagination and consider the feelings that arise within you as you meditate on this encounter.

‡ Reflect on the emotions that fill the hearts of Abram, Sarai, and Hagar in this scene. What are the feelings that seem to predominate in the heart of each of them?

‡ In what ways did Sarai's plan for surrogate motherhood create a triangle of trouble? What allows triangles of trouble to form in relationships and families?

‡ How does the text demonstrate that Hagar is uniquely blessed by God? What did God's messenger promise her? What is surprising about these blessings?

Oratio

None of your emotions can be hidden from God, and in fact, emotions can be most useful in promoting a spirit of honest prayer.

> Lord, you are the God who truly sees me. You know the emotional conflicts that rage within me: generosity, jealousy, anger, and hope. Help me to trust in your plan for my life and my family.

Continue to pray to God through the emotions that fill your heart . . .

Contemplatio

Seek to experience the unconditional love that God demonstrated for Hagar, the foreign slave. Know that God has the same unrestricted love for you. Spend some moments seeking to feel that kind of love from God.

After your time of contemplation, write a few words about your experience.

Operatio

How is God's Word in this text transforming my heart? How can I better use my emotions to be more honest with God in prayer and more genuine in my daily actions?

7

Ancestor of a
Multitude of Nations

Lectio

Highlight or underline passages that seem most significant as you read the
Scriptures and commentary. These marks will help you ask questions of the
text and seek to understand its significance.

GENESIS 17:1–14

[1]When Abram was ninety-nine years old, the LORD appeared to
Abram, and said to him, "I am God Almighty; walk before me, and
be blameless. [2]And I will make my covenant between me and you,
and will make you exceedingly numerous." [3]Then Abram fell on
his face; and God said to him, [4]"As for me, this is my covenant with
you: You shall be the ancestor of a multitude of nations. [5]No longer
shall your name be Abram, but your name shall be Abraham; for I
have made you the ancestor of a multitude of nations. [6]I will make
you exceedingly fruitful; and I will make nations of you, and kings
shall come from you. [7]I will establish my covenant between me and
you, and your offspring after you throughout their generations, for
an everlasting covenant, to be God to you and to your offspring after
you. [8]And I will give to you, and to your offspring after you, the land

where you are now an alien, all the land of Canaan, for a perpetual holding; and I will be their God."

⁹God said to Abraham, "As for you, you shall keep my covenant, you and your offspring after you throughout their generations. ¹⁰This is my covenant, which you shall keep, between me and you and your offspring after you: Every male among you shall be circumcised. ¹¹You shall circumcise the flesh of your foreskins, and it shall be a sign of the covenant between me and you. ¹²Throughout your generations every male among you shall be circumcised when he is eight days old, including the slave born in your house and the one bought with your money from any foreigner who is not of your offspring. ¹³Both the slave born in your house and the one bought with your money must be circumcised. So shall my covenant be in your flesh an everlasting covenant. ¹⁴Any uncircumcised male who is not circumcised in the flesh of his foreskin shall be cut off from his people; he has broken my covenant."

Continue seeking to understand this Scripture passage through the help of these remarks:

Twenty-four years after Abram left Haran and thirteen years after the birth of Ishmael, God's promises still remained unfulfilled. Again God appeared to Abram, this time identified as God Almighty (in Hebrew, *El Shaddai*). The word "covenant" appears ten times in these verses, and the covenant is redefined as an "everlasting covenant." In the earlier covenant making (Gen. 15), God was the active partner and Abram the passive recipient of God's promises. Here God asks for a commitment from Abram and summons him to be an active partner in the covenant: "Walk before me, and be blameless" (v. 1). Abram is told to live with an awareness of God's presence and to behave with integrity. In an expression of awe and submission to God, Abram falls prostrate with his face to the ground (v. 3).

Through the covenant, Abram will be "the ancestor of a multitude of nations" (vv. 4–5). This implies that Abram will be the father of nations other than Israel. Through his son Ishmael and his future son Isaac, Abram will become the father of two great peoples. Furthermore, Abram will generate an increasingly large segment of humanity that looks upon him as its spiritual ancestor. This expanded role for the patriarch is expressed through the expansion of his name, from Abram ("exalted father") to Abraham ("father of multitudes"; v. 5). A change of names in the Bible signifies a change in a person's character or destiny. The results of God's promises and Abraham's fidelity will unfold generation after generation, as Abraham's offspring grow into "nations" and "kings" who honor God (vv. 6–7).

As part of the active response to the divine promises, God commands that every male of Abraham's household and of his descendants be circumcised as "a sign of the covenant" (v. 11). The practice of circumcising the foreskins of males was a common practice among the peoples of the ancient Middle East. Abraham needed no explanation or instruction. Yet among other peoples the practice was almost always associated with puberty and preparation for marriage. By commanding circumcision on the eighth day after birth, God fundamentally transformed its meaning. It became the sign and seal of trust in God's promises and entrance into the covenant. As a physical and permanent mark "in the flesh," circumcision symbolized the bearer's enduring, irrevocable commitment to the covenant with God (vv. 12–13).

Now that you have read the text and commentary carefully, answer these questions:

⸸ What is the significance of changing Abram's name to Abraham at this moment?

⸸ Why is circumcision such an effective "sign of the covenant" (v. 11)?

Meditatio

Consider what God is teaching you through this Scripture passage and what personal message God wants you to understand.

‡ In what aspect of my life have I had to wait a long time for the fulfillment of God's promises? Is there a value in waiting?

‡ Abraham became an active partner with God in the covenant. In what ways has Abraham become the ancestor of "a multitude of nations" (v. 4)? What are the challenges today among the descendants of Abraham in keeping this covenant with God?

‡ If circumcision is no longer required in the Christian tradition for initiation into the covenant, what is now required (see Gal. 5:6)? What other identity markers demonstrate my religious faith?

Oratio

After listening to God speak to you through the words of Scripture, respond to God with whatever words arise within you.

> God Almighty, you have invited me to walk in your presence. Give me the patience to wait for the fulfillment of your pledges. Give me the grace to leave a legacy for future generations.

Speak words that express whatever new hope or purpose you have discovered . . .

Contemplatio

When words cease to be helpful in prayer, simply relax in God's presence. Do nothing, say nothing. Just trust in our faithful God who promises you a future full of hope.

Following your contemplative prayer, write a few words describing your experience.

Operatio

God's Word shapes our future and offers us hope. What new hope and renewed sense of mission have I received from my dialogue with God through this Scripture?

8

Falling Down Laughing

Lectio

Dismiss the distractions of the day and enter into a quiet space where you can listen to God's voice speak through the literary text. As you read, allow yourself to feel the physical and emotional aspects of the covenant God made with Abram and Sarai.

GENESIS 17:15–27

15God said to Abraham, "As for Sarai your wife, you shall not call her Sarai, but Sarah shall be her name. 16I will bless her, and moreover I will give you a son by her. I will bless her, and she shall give rise to nations; kings of peoples shall come from her." 17Then Abraham fell on his face and laughed, and said to himself, "Can a child be born to a man who is a hundred years old? Can Sarah, who is ninety years old, bear a child?" 18And Abraham said to God, "O that Ishmael might live in your sight!" 19God said, "No, but your wife Sarah shall bear you a son, and you shall name him Isaac. I will establish my covenant with him as an everlasting covenant for his offspring after him. 20As for Ishmael, I have heard you; I will bless him and make him fruitful and exceedingly numerous; he shall be the father of twelve princes, and I will make him a great nation. 21But my covenant I will establish with Isaac, whom Sarah shall bear to you at this season next year." 22And when he had finished talking with him, God went up from Abraham.

²³Then Abraham took his son Ishmael and all the slaves born in his house or bought with his money, every male among the men of Abraham's house, and he circumcised the flesh of their foreskins that very day, as God had said to him. ²⁴Abraham was ninety-nine years old when he was circumcised in the flesh of his foreskin. ²⁵And his son Ishmael was thirteen years old when he was circumcised in the flesh of his foreskin. ²⁶That very day Abraham and his son Ishmael were circumcised; ²⁷and all the men of his house, slaves born in the house and those bought with money from a foreigner, were circumcised with him.

After allowing this Scripture to enter your mind and resonate in your body, continue your exploration through this commentary.

As God continued to reveal his plan, Sarai, too, is given a new name, Sarah, signifying her new destiny. God will end her infertility and give her a son. No longer will she be a barren woman; she will be the mother of nations, and kings of different peoples will come from her (vv. 15–16).

Abraham was so bowled over by God's incredible words that he broke out laughing (v. 17). We are not told whether Abraham's laugh was from surprise, skepticism, mockery, or joy. Perhaps it was a mixture of all of these, the spontaneous laughter that arises when one seeks to avoid being overwhelmed by a confusing cacophony of sudden feelings. The blessing given to Sarah seemed impossible, so Abraham tried to redirect God's attention to Ishmael (v. 18). Hadn't this already been settled? Wasn't Ishmael the heir to the covenant? God assured Abraham that Ishmael would indeed be blessed: he would be the father of twelve princes who would become a great nation (v. 20). But Sarah's son, Isaac, will inherit the covenant.

The name Isaac comes from the Hebrew root for "laughter." Every time Abraham would hear his son's name in the future, he would be reminded of God's incredible, laughable ways. After Abraham had waited for so many years for Sarah to have a child, hoping against the evidence, God asked him to believe for just one more year (v. 21). Isaac, forevermore, would represent the triumph of God's power over human limitations and doubt.

Immediately Abraham obeyed God, circumcising Ishmael, all males of his household and among his servants, and even himself, at age ninety-nine (vv. 23–27). Through the ritual of circumcision, the covenant would be renewed in each new generation. By performing the rite of circumcision, each child's father acknowledged God's role in the conception and birth of his son, renewing his own covenant with God and marking the starting point of his child's spiritual journey.

The fact that only men bear the sign of the covenant on their bodies should not be viewed as evidence that women have an inferior relationship to God's covenant. A woman's entire body is involved in the conception, birth, and nursing of a child, linking her to her mother and her children and affirming her connection with the Creator. Men have a much more tenuous connection to the mystery of bringing forth new life. The mark of circumcision creates the awareness that a man's sexuality is central to his spiritual identity. The ritual intensifies men's connections to their fathers and their sons, and it heightens their sense of responsibility to raise their children in God's path and to play a personal role in their children's upbringing.

In the Christian tradition, the ancestral rite of circumcision illuminates the practice of baptism. Like circumcision for the Jewish people, baptism is an entrance into a new life and signifies loyalty to a community. The Jewish sign of the covenant became the model for the life of Christian faith through baptism, "a spiritual circumcision," "the circumcision of Christ" (Col. 2:11–13).

Continue to listen for God's voice in Scripture and answer these questions:

‡ Why does Abraham try to redirect God's attention toward Ishmael (v. 18)?

‡ Why is circumcision a ritual that marks the relationship between fathers and sons?

Meditatio

Spend some time seeking to personalize the text you have just read, asking yourself what the passage means to you.

‡ What emotions might Abraham have felt when told that he and Sarah would have a son? What caused Abraham's laughter?

‡ Why is Isaac's name so appropriate? When have I laughed when I didn't know what else to do? Do I ever associate laughter with God's revealing presence and sacred events?

‡ In what ways is the Jewish ritual of circumcision similar to the Christian sacrament of baptism?

Oratio

Choose the words or phrases from this passage that have most clearly spoken to your heart. Use these words as the foundation of your own heartfelt prayer to God.

> God of Abraham and Sarah, you are eternally faithful to your people. The wonders you work for us are amazing. Help me to trust you when I am besieged by doubts and fears about the future.

Continue to pray from your heart using the words and ideas of the Scriptures . . .

Contemplatio

Choose a word from the text to ponder. Allow this word to help you focus. When you get distracted in your silent prayer, use that word to bring you back into focus.

After your experience of contemplative prayer, write a few words describing this encounter with God.

Operatio

Abraham acted on the word he received from God. What must I do to remain faithful to God's offer of covenant with me? What does God want me to do today to be obedient to him?

9

Abraham Hosts
the Strangers

Lectio

Place yourself amid the sights, sounds, smells, tastes, and textures through-out this scene. Use your imagination to experience the life within the text.

GENESIS 18:1–15

¹The LORD appeared to Abraham by the oaks of Mamre, as he sat at the entrance of his tent in the heat of the day. ²He looked up and saw three men standing near him. When he saw them, he ran from the tent entrance to meet them, and bowed down to the ground. ³He said, "My lord, if I find favor with you, do not pass by your servant. ⁴Let a little water be brought, and wash your feet, and rest yourselves under the tree. ⁵Let me bring a little bread, that you may refresh yourselves, and after that you may pass on—since you have come to your servant." So they said, "Do as you have said." ⁶And Abraham hastened into the tent to Sarah, and said, "Make ready quickly three measures of choice flour, knead it, and make cakes." ⁷Abraham ran to the herd, and took a calf, tender and good, and gave it to the servant, who hastened to prepare it. ⁸Then he took curds and milk and the calf that he had prepared, and set it before them; and he stood by them under the tree while they ate.

⁹They said to him, "Where is your wife Sarah?" And he said, "There, in the tent." ¹⁰Then one said, "I will surely return to you in due season, and your wife Sarah shall have a son." And Sarah was listening at the tent entrance behind him. ¹¹Now Abraham and Sarah were old, advanced in age; it had ceased to be with Sarah after the manner of women. ¹²So Sarah laughed to herself, saying, "After I have grown old, and my husband is old, shall I have pleasure?" ¹³The LORD said to Abraham, "Why did Sarah laugh, and say, 'Shall I indeed bear a child, now that I am old?' ¹⁴Is anything too wonderful for the LORD? At the set time I will return to you, in due season, and Sarah shall have a son." ¹⁵But Sarah denied, saying, "I did not laugh"; for she was afraid. He said, "Oh yes, you did laugh."

Continue searching for the full significance of this scene by considering these comments.

One of the worst casualties of our fast-paced, media-driven culture is the ancient virtue of hospitality. We are losing the art of opening our homes in welcome, graciously attending to the needs of guests, and leisurely sharing meals with others. In the biblical world, such graciousness was an honored virtue. The rabbis taught that we draw closest to God not through isolated prayer or sacrificial worship but through personally tending to the everyday needs of others. As the Talmud says, "Hospitality to wayfarers is greater than welcoming the Divine Presence."

Abraham's tent, set in the shade of the oak trees at Mamre, was a hospitable place for travelers. Abraham honored his three guests by offering them a place of rest and refreshment in the noonday heat. His openhearted cordiality knew no bounds. Offering to bring his guests "a little bread," he prepared a feast for them. Bread made of finest flour, curds and milk, and a choice, tender calf made a first-rate spread to place before his guests.

Apparently Abraham does not, at first, think there is anything extraordinary about these three travelers. Rather, he responds in character to the strangers, demonstrating that he recognizes the presence of God in everyone he meets. The narrator, however, clues in the reader from the beginning that this is a divine visit (v. 1). It is only when the strangers ask about Sarah by name and reveal the extraordinary news of her maternity that there are any clues that Abraham understands he has been entertaining messengers from God (vv. 9–10).

Listening from inside the tent, Sarah hears that by this time next year she will have a son. She is so flabbergasted at the silliness of the message that she laughs to herself (v. 12). She wonders how she and her husband can possibly experience sexual pleasure and conceive a child. Like Abraham in the previous scene (17:17), Sarah laughs because she doesn't know how else to respond to a suggestion that seems so absurd. Yet, when challenged about her laughter by the messenger, Sarah denies laughing because she is embarrassed and afraid (v. 15). The name of her son, Isaac ("he laughs"), will continually remind her of the unpredictable, even humorous ways that God keeps his promises.

The key question of the passage, however, is not about laughter but about the astonishing ways of God: "Is anything too wonderful for the LORD?" (v. 14). The question really is an invitation to faith. Is God's power limited to our expectations of life, or can we dare to believe that God will keep his astounding promises to us? Faith is not a reasonable act that fits into the normal scheme of life but rather the ability to put our trust in what sometimes seems laughable.

After reading the Scripture and commentary, answer these questions to help focus your thoughts:

✣ What indicates the lavishness of Abraham's hospitality to strangers?

✣ What is so wondrous about God's promises to Abraham and Sarah?

Meditatio

Try to personalize God's message by allowing this passage to resonate with your own hopes and dreams.

‡ What does Abraham teach me about hospitality? How can I imitate him?

‡ The letter to the Hebrews says: "Do not neglect to show hospitality to strangers, for by doing that some have entertained angels without knowing it" (Heb. 13:2). What does this verse mean to me?

‡ "Is anything too wonderful for the Lᴏʀᴅ?" (v. 14). How do I respond to this question? What is the most wonderful promise God has made to me?

Oratio

Speak these words of prayer in response to God, whom you have heard in the Scriptures:

> Lord God, every person is created in your image and contains a spark of your divine life. Help me to see your face in the people I meet, especially in the wayfarer and the stranger.

Continue praying to God using the words that come to you after meditating on this passage . . .

Contemplatio

God's promises to us are wonderful. Spend a few moments of silence basking in the love of the One for whom nothing is too wonderful.

Spend a few moments writing about your contemplative prayer.

Operatio

Faith is the ability to believe in divine promises that go far beyond our reasonable expectations. How has my faith in God's astounding promises been deepened after pondering these inspired Scriptures?

10

Abraham Intercedes for Sodom

 Lectio

Read this familiar passage as if for the first time. Listen to God's Word in the text while considering God's way of dealing with Sodom and Gomorrah.

GENESIS 18:16–33

[16]Then the men set out from there, and they looked toward Sodom; and Abraham went with them to set them on their way. [17]The LORD said, "Shall I hide from Abraham what I am about to do, [18]seeing that Abraham shall become a great and mighty nation, and all the nations of the earth shall be blessed in him? [19]No, for I have chosen him, that he may charge his children and his household after him to keep the way of the LORD by doing righteousness and justice; so that the LORD may bring about for Abraham what he has promised him." [20]Then the LORD said, "How great is the outcry against Sodom and Gomorrah and how very grave their sin! [21]I must go down and see whether they have done altogether according to the outcry that has come to me; and if not, I will know."

[22]So the men turned from there, and went toward Sodom, while Abraham remained standing before the LORD. [23]Then Abraham came near and said, "Will you indeed sweep away the righteous with the wicked? [24]Suppose there are fifty righteous within the city; will you then

sweep away the place and not forgive it for the fifty righteous who are in it? ²⁵Far be it from you to do such a thing, to slay the righteous with the wicked, so that the righteous fare as the wicked! Far be that from you! Shall not the Judge of all the earth do what is just?" ²⁶And the LORD said, "If I find at Sodom fifty righteous in the city, I will forgive the whole place for their sake." ²⁷Abraham answered, "Let me take it upon myself to speak to the LORD, I who am but dust and ashes. ²⁸Suppose five of the fifty righteous are lacking? Will you destroy the whole city for lack of five?" And he said, "I will not destroy it if I find forty-five there." ²⁹Again he spoke to him, "Suppose forty are found there." He answered, "For the sake of forty I will not do it." ³⁰Then he said, "Oh do not let the LORD be angry if I speak. Suppose thirty are found there." He answered, "I will not do it, if I find thirty there." ³¹He said, "Let me take it upon myself to speak to the LORD. Suppose twenty are found there." He answered, "For the sake of twenty I will not destroy it." ³²Then he said, "Oh do not let the LORD be angry if I speak just once more. Suppose ten are found there." He answered, "For the sake of ten I will not destroy it." ³³And the LORD went his way, when he had finished speaking to Abraham; and Abraham returned to his place.

After listening to this passage with the ear of your heart, continue pondering the text through these remarks:

The divine messengers continue their journey, looking toward Sodom, their next destination. Abraham, always the hospitable host, walks along with them to see them on their way (v. 16). God wonders if he should tell Abraham about the mission of his messengers: to determine whether or not divine judgment should be executed on the sinful cities of Sodom and Gomorrah (vv. 17, 20–21). In deciding to inform Abraham about the mission of his messengers, God reiterates that "all the nations of the earth shall be blessed in him" (v. 18; 12:3). God's message reveals the divine will that Abraham and his descendants mediate for other peoples, especially those under judgment, and in that way become a source of blessings for other nations. As bearer of God's promises toward all peoples, Abraham and his progeny would have the privilege of interceding for the sake of others in the interactive relationship God desires between himself and human beings.

The sin and punishment of Sodom and Gomorrah have transformed the names of those cities into permanent reminders of human wickedness and divine judgment. God describes his judgment of the city with two exclamations: "How great is the outcry against Sodom and Gomorrah and how very grave their sin!" (v. 20). An "outcry" in the Bible is usually a plea by those suffering from oppression, a cry to heaven with hope that God will rescue them. The sin, it seems, is social corruption: an arrogant disregard for basic human rights and a cynical insensitivity to the sufferings of others (Jer. 23:14; Ezek. 16:49). God was going there to see if the volume of the outcry corresponded with the reality of the oppression.

Abraham stands before God to plead on behalf of the pagan people of Sodom. He decides to appeal for God to save the wicked city of Sodom based on the merits of an innocent minority. Thinking that God must be a harsh and calculating judge like the gods of the surrounding nations, Abraham prepares to plead and bargain with God. Abraham first chooses the number fifty as his bartering figure: save the city on behalf of fifty righteous people (v. 24). He purposely chose a low number, thinking that in the typical bargaining style, God would choose a much higher number, and then they would meet somewhere in the middle. But Abraham's strategy is undone by God's immediate acceptance of his offer. Lowering the offer to forty-five, forty, thirty, twenty, and finally ten, Abraham discovers that God is far more merciful than he had imagined.

Although Sodom is destroyed (Gen. 19), apparently because not even ten righteous people could be found there, God does save the family of Lot. Through his experience, Abraham learned "the way of the LORD" (v. 19), the way of justice, righteousness, and mercy that characterizes God's actions among his creation. God does not judge by the usual moralism, in which people simply receive their due. God is not a scorekeeper, always ready to pounce and punish; rather, God is far more ready to forgive and to celebrate the goodness of a few. In this way, Abraham is able to teach God's way to his posterity. As the Talmud observes, "Whoever is merciful to his fellow human beings is without doubt of the children of our father Abraham." God wants his people to boldly appeal to him, to plead for others who are hurting or in sin. When God is approached with genuine concern and pure motives, he is moved by intercessory prayer.

Meditatio

Think about what God is teaching you in this passage about "the way of the
LORD." *Consider what you are learning about living God's ways.*

‡ Do I ever try to bargain with God? What are the pros and cons of this
type of negotiating with God? How does God challenge Abraham's as-
sumptions about the way God works?

‡ What is most surprising about God's response to Abraham's bargaining?
How does Abraham's experience challenge me to doubt and question
my routine ways of thinking about God?

‡ Abraham's courageous intercession for the people of Sodom teaches us
not to be passive spectators in the face of the world's challenges but to
intercede with active compassion. In what ways am I able to intercede
for other people before God?

Oratio

Pray for the gift of mercy and compassion, that your own heart might reflect the heart of God.

God of justice and mercy, you demonstrate that you are always ready to forgive and welcome us back to you. Teach me your ways so that I can make your compassion known to others. Give me an active concern for the people of our world.

Continue to intercede before God for the people of the world . . .

Contemplatio

Remain in quiet and stillness, allowing the unfathomable God of Abraham to be your God. Let divine compassion radiate from within you.

Write a few words about your experience of contemplative prayer.

Operatio

Lectio divina is a way of letting God's Word shape us and change us. How have I been molded and transformed by the Word of God in this Scripture?

11

Abraham and Sarah
at Gerar

Lectio

Listen to the words of Scripture as you read them aloud. Pay attention to the emotive force behind the spoken words, and let God's Word teach you his ways.

GENESIS 20:1–18

¹From there Abraham journeyed toward the region of the Negeb, and settled between Kadesh and Shur. While residing in Gerar as an alien, ²Abraham said of his wife Sarah, "She is my sister." And King Abimelech of Gerar sent and took Sarah. ³But God came to Abimelech in a dream by night, and said to him, "You are about to die because of the woman whom you have taken; for she is a married woman." ⁴Now Abimelech had not approached her; so he said, "Lord, will you destroy an innocent people? ⁵Did he not himself say to me, 'She is my sister'? And she herself said, 'He is my brother.' I did this in the integrity of my heart and the innocence of my hands." ⁶Then God said to him in the dream, "Yes, I know that you did this in the integrity of your heart; furthermore it was I who kept you from sinning against me. Therefore I did not let you touch her. ⁷Now then, return the man's wife; for he is a prophet, and he will pray for you and you shall live. But if you do not restore her, know that you shall surely die, you and all that are yours."

⁸So Abimelech rose early in the morning, and called all his servants and told them all these things; and the men were very much afraid. ⁹Then Abimelech called Abraham, and said to him, "What have you done to us? How have I sinned against you, that you have brought such great guilt on me and my kingdom? You have done things to me that ought not to be done." ¹⁰And Abimelech said to Abraham, "What were you thinking of, that you did this thing?" ¹¹Abraham said, "I did it because I thought, There is no fear of God at all in this place, and they will kill me because of my wife. ¹²Besides, she is indeed my sister, the daughter of my father but not the daughter of my mother; and she became my wife. ¹³And when God caused me to wander from my father's house, I said to her, 'This is the kindness you must do me: at every place to which we come, say of me, He is my brother.'" ¹⁴Then Abimelech took sheep and oxen, and male and female slaves, and gave them to Abraham, and restored his wife Sarah to him. ¹⁵Abimelech said, "My land is before you; settle where it pleases you." ¹⁶To Sarah he said, "Look, I have given your brother a thousand pieces of silver; it is your exoneration before all who are with you; you are completely vindicated." ¹⁷Then Abraham prayed to God; and God healed Abimelech, and also healed his wife and female slaves so that they bore children. ¹⁸For the Lord had closed fast all the wombs of the house of Abimelech because of Sarah, Abraham's wife.

Continue listening for the fuller purpose of this Scripture passage in God's plan of revelation.

Abraham and Sarah resumed their wanderings through the Promised Land, traveling to its southernmost limits, the oasis of Kadesh and the Egyptian fortress of Shur. They then entered the royal city of Gerar, perhaps for the purpose of trade in the city. Fearing for his own life, Abraham again resorted to the strategy of introducing Sarah as his sister, the same ploy he had used in Egypt (v. 2; 12:10–20). Again, Sarah is taken into the king's harem, but she is saved from dishonor by God's intervention.

We are not told why King Abimelech took Sarah into the royal family. The Jewish midrash comments that with the promise of a child, God had restored not only Sarah's childbearing capacity but her youthful beauty as well. It is quite possible, however, that Abimelech wanted to form an economically advantageous alliance with Abraham through marriage to his "sister."

God then revealed to Abimelech in a dream that he was under the threat of death because of his abduction of a married woman (v. 3). But, defending his innocence, Abimelech argued on two grounds: he had not "approached her," another way of saying he did not have sexual relations with her, and he was not aware of her married status, since he had been told she was Abraham's sister (vv. 4–5).

Abimelech's dialogue with God revolves around the theme of justice—whether God would destroy innocent people—as does Abraham's dialogue with God about the city of Sodom (vv. 4–7; 18:16–33). The king of Gerar and his people are saved through the prayers of Abraham (vv. 7, 17), just as Lot was saved. In both narratives, Abraham was the intercessor before God on behalf of others. Here God describes Abraham as a "prophet," the first use of this term in the Bible. In this role, Abraham is not only a spokesperson for God but also a mediator between God and other people. He prays that Abimelech might be healed and live.

Deeply affected by his dream, the king summons his officials, who are very fearful about the matter (v. 8). Confronted by Abimelech, Abraham offers a feeble explanation (vv. 9–13). Though portrayed as far less than righteous, Abraham nevertheless emerges with his authority and his riches enhanced, and the king tells him he may dwell wherever he wishes (vv. 14–16). The pre-eminence of Abraham rests not on his own virtues but on God's promise.

Following your reading of the Scripture and commentary, answer these questions:

‡ In what ways does this passage show Abraham to be less than virtuous?

‡ How does Abimelech act more honorably than Abraham in this account?

Meditatio

Use your imagination and enter the scene. Reflect on these questions:

‡ What do I think about the significance of dreams? Could God still reveal his will to people in dreams? What dream has taught me something about myself and what God might want for me?

‡ In what aspects of this account do I most identify with Abraham? Doubting God's promises? Needing to be rescued from my own mistakes? Making the same mistake again?

‡ In what ways does this passage show that God's grace overcomes human frailty and faithlessness? How have I seen God's grace working in this way in my own life?

Oratio

Respond in prayer to God, who knows you intimately and continues to forgive you and provide for your good.

> Mighty God, for the sake of your promises you heal our human faults and infidelity. Show me how to be an intercessor for others, praying to you for their healing and forgiveness.

Continue to pray for forgiveness for yourself and others . . .

Contemplatio

Imagine what it would be like to believe in God's complete forgiveness. Rest in silence, confident in God's healing compassion.

Write a few words about your experience of trusting in God's mercy.

Operatio

In what way does my experience of God's merciful pardon lead me to want to forgive others? How can I forgive someone today?

12

Laughing with Sarah
at Isaac's Birth

Lectio

Joyfully speak the words of the sacred text aloud. Read the text with your eyes and hear it with your ears.

GENESIS 21:1–7

> ¹The LORD dealt with Sarah as he had said, and the LORD did for Sarah as he had promised. ²Sarah conceived and bore Abraham a son in his old age, at the time of which God had spoken to him. ³Abraham gave the name Isaac to his son whom Sarah bore him. ⁴And Abraham circumcised his son Isaac when he was eight days old, as God had commanded him. ⁵Abraham was a hundred years old when his son Isaac was born to him. ⁶Now Sarah said, "God has brought laughter for me; everyone who hears will laugh with me." ⁷And she said, "Who would ever have said to Abraham that Sarah would nurse children? Yet I have borne him a son in his old age."

While enjoying the delight of this narrative, continue seeking to understand the full significance of the text in God's saving plan.

God keeps his word. If there is any message that comes through clearly in the Abraham narratives, it is that God is faithful in keeping his promises: "The LORD did for Sarah as he had promised" (v. 1). But God's promises are not delivered according to our timetable. The text tells us that Abraham was a hundred years old when his son Isaac was born (v. 5). A full quarter century had passed since he first heard God's call promising him innumerable descendants. The stance of the believer, then, in awaiting the fulfillment of God's promises after the example of Abraham, is patient expectation.

The birth of Isaac is the culmination of a history of obstacles and disappointments. The Abraham narratives up to this point have described a series of crises that threatened to make the fulfillment of divine promises impossible. Yet the brief narrative of Isaac's birth describes matter-of-factly that indeed God's Word has come to fruition. The child's birth is the resolution of all the anxious waiting, worries, and doubts. This brief passage is the perfect portrait and ideal model for God's faithfulness. Each detail describes how the expectations of the previous narratives find their completion in Isaac's birth. Sarah bore Abraham a son according to the schedule the divine messengers had relayed, "at the time of which God had spoken to him" (v. 2; see 18:14). Abraham named his son Isaac, as God had previously directed him (v. 3; 17:19), and he circumcised his son on the eighth day after his birth, just as God had decreed (v. 4; 17:12). Isaac is the first person circumcised according to God's timetable, after seven days of life, emphasizing Isaac's role as the true heir to the covenant.

This newborn son is so appropriately named: Isaac—he laughs. Sarah says, "God has brought laughter for me" (v. 6). Laughter seems the appropriate response to a newness that cannot be reasonably explained. Through his Word and promise, God has broken the sullen grip of barrenness and hopelessness. The promised son is a work of pure grace—an unearned, undeserved gift. Sarah's earlier laugh of embarrassed skepticism (18:12–15) now becomes joyous, unrestrained laughter. It is a contagious laughter that will spread to all who hear the news of Isaac's birth. Sarah is glad that everyone who hears will laugh along with her.

Now that you have listened to God's Word in the Scriptures, answer these questions about the text:

✝ In what ways does the text reveal that God is both faithful and unpredictable?

✝ How does this narrative describe the relationship between divine and human faithfulness?

✝ Why is "Laughter" such a perfect name for Sarah's child?

✝ What is the relationship between joyful laughter and God's grace?

✝ Why is patient expectation the necessary stance of every believer?

Meditatio

Reflect on the text from the viewpoint of Abraham and Sarah. Try to experience the situation and make their feelings your own.

✝ What are other examples of God's pure grace in the Bible? What is an unearned gift that I have received from God?

✝ Why might God delay the fulfillment of his promises to us? What is the longest I have had to wait for God to act? Have I ever seen advantages in relying on God's timetable rather than my own?

✝ In what ways is Sarah's laughter contagious? What does joyful laughter have to do with a relationship with God? When have I experienced the presence of God through laughter?

Oratio

After engaging your emotions in this passage, respond to God with words that arise from your heart. Pray in these or similar words.

Lord God, I am grateful for the unearned gifts you have given me. Give me the gift of faith so that I may trust in you completely, the gift of hope that I may look to the future with confidence, and the gift of laughter that I may rejoice in your grace.

Continue to pray to God with the joy and hope that arise from within you . . .

Contemplatio

Relax, place a smile on your face, and ask God for the gift of joyfulness. Rest in the presence of the God who wants you to experience happiness and laughter.

Write a few words about this contemplative experience.

Operatio

How has Abraham changed through his experiences of God? How is God shaping my approach to life and my outlook as a result of my lectio divina?

13

Banishment of Hagar
and Ishmael

Lectio

Read the Scripture slowly while considering the sorrowful scene and the
painful emotions of Sarah and Hagar.

GENESIS 21:8–21

⁸The child grew, and was weaned; and Abraham made a great feast
on the day that Isaac was weaned. ⁹But Sarah saw the son of Hagar the
Egyptian, whom she had borne to Abraham, playing with her son Isaac.
¹⁰So she said to Abraham, "Cast out this slave woman with her son; for
the son of this slave woman shall not inherit along with my son Isaac."
¹¹The matter was very distressing to Abraham on account of his son.
¹²But God said to Abraham, "Do not be distressed because of the boy
and because of your slave woman; whatever Sarah says to you, do as she
tells you, for it is through Isaac that offspring shall be named for you.
¹³As for the son of the slave woman, I will make a nation of him also,
because he is your offspring." ¹⁴So Abraham rose early in the morning,
and took bread and a skin of water, and gave it to Hagar, putting it on
her shoulder, along with the child, and sent her away. And she departed,
and wandered about in the wilderness of Beer-sheba.

¹⁵When the water in the skin was gone, she cast the child under one of the bushes. ¹⁶Then she went and sat down opposite him a good way off, about the distance of a bowshot; for she said, "Do not let me look on the death of the child." And as she sat opposite him, she lifted up her voice and wept. ¹⁷And God heard the voice of the boy; and the angel of God called to Hagar from heaven, and said to her, "What troubles you, Hagar? Do not be afraid; for God has heard the voice of the boy where he is. ¹⁸Come, lift up the boy and hold him fast with your hand, for I will make a great nation of him." ¹⁹Then God opened her eyes and she saw a well of water. She went, and filled the skin with water, and gave the boy a drink. ²⁰God was with the boy, and he grew up; he lived in the wilderness, and became an expert with the bow. ²¹He lived in the wilderness of Paran; and his mother got a wife for him from the land of Egypt.

After reading this passage with your mind and your heart, continue searching for its meaning through this commentary.

The joyful laughter of Isaac's birth is soon overshadowed by the sad family discord that began on the feast of Isaac's weaning. Because infant mortality was so high in Canaanite culture, families celebrated a child's survival of infancy and the beginning of childhood's next stage by throwing a feast at the child's weaning, usually around the age of two or three (v. 8). The conflict began when Sarah saw the son of Hagar "playing" with her son, Isaac (v. 9). The word translated here as "playing" can also mean "mocking," "making fun of," or "fooling around." Considering that Ishmael was the older brother of Isaac, such conduct should not be surprising.

Sarah became protective when she saw Ishmael's behavior, and she pleaded with Abraham to banish "this slave woman with her son" (v. 10). Legally it seems that Ishmael held the inheritance rights as Abraham's firstborn son. The key to understanding Sarah's demand is the legal clause that allows a father to grant freedom to a slave woman and the children she has borne him, in which case they give up their share of inherited property (see Judg. 11:1–3). Sarah was insisting that Abraham release Hagar and Ishmael so that they forfeit any inheritance.

Abraham was in great distress over the emotional conflict between fatherly love for his firstborn and loyalty to his beloved wife (v. 11). Yet God prompted Abraham to agree to Sarah's demands based on two assurances: first, God tells Abraham that his line will continue through Isaac, and second, God has other plans in mind for Ishmael, plans that will give him a great future (vv. 12–13). So reluctantly Abraham packed food and water for Hagar and sent her away with Ishmael the next day (v. 14).

Though Hagar and Ishmael were presumably heading in the direction of Hagar's native Egypt, she lost her way and began to wander frantically in the wilderness. When the water was consumed and they were in danger of death in the desert, Hagar and her son cried out to God in desperation. God heard their cry and sent a word of hope through the voice of a divine messenger. The angel instructed her to lift up the boy because God was going to make him into "a great nation" (v. 18).

The stories of the two sons are juxtaposed. As in the parable of the prodigal son told by Jesus, the older son pleases his father, obeys the rules, and deserves honor, but the younger son is celebrated. God honors both sons of Abraham, and the text does not force us to choose one or the other. God remembers both of Abraham's children. While Isaac is celebrated, God remembers Ishmael, offering him water in the wilderness and assurances of a noble future.

Now that you have read the stories of Isaac and Ishmael, answer these questions about the text:

✝ For what reasons might Sarah have demanded that Abraham banish Hagar and Ishmael?

✝ What reassurance does God offer to Hagar in her anguish?

Meditatio

Reflect on how the inspired text speaks God's Word to the circumstances of your own life.

‡ What are some of the emotional conflicts adults feel between love for their children and love for their spouse? In what ways are these emotions intensified and complicated in blended families that include children, stepchildren, spouses, and ex-spouses?

‡ In what ways does this account reflect the emotional struggles involved in blended families. What dos and don'ts can I learn from this episode for achieving the sensitive balance required in blended families today?

‡ What parallels do I see between this narrative of Abraham's two sons and the parable of the two sons told by Jesus (Luke 15:11–32)?

Oratio

Speak to God in response to the words, ideas, and images from the reading. Use these or similar words.

God of our fathers and mothers, you called Abraham, Hagar, and Sarah to be the patriarch and matriarchs of great peoples and nations. Help me to live a life worthy of the great legacy I have been given by my ancestors, and help me to pass on my faith to the next generation.

Continue to respond to God, who has first spoken to you . . .

Contemplatio

When God's people lift up their voices and call out to God, he listens and comes to them. In wordless silence, receptively allow God to fill your heart with his divine presence.

Write a few words about your experience of God in silence.

Operatio

The angel of God tells Hagar, "Do not be afraid" (v. 17). What fears does God wish to alleviate from my life? How could fearlessness affect the way I live today?

14

Abraham's Well
at Beer-sheba

Lectio

In a quiet place, read the Scripture carefully, asking God's Spirit to guide your understanding.

GENESIS 21:22–34

²²At that time Abimelech, with Phicol the commander of his army, said to Abraham, "God is with you in all that you do; ²³now therefore swear to me here by God that you will not deal falsely with me or with my offspring or with my posterity, but as I have dealt loyally with you, you will deal with me and with the land where you have resided as an alien." ²⁴And Abraham said, "I swear it."

²⁵When Abraham complained to Abimelech about a well of water that Abimelech's servants had seized, ²⁶Abimelech said, "I do not know who has done this; you did not tell me, and I have not heard of it until today." ²⁷So Abraham took sheep and oxen and gave them to Abimelech, and the two men made a covenant. ²⁸Abraham set apart seven ewe lambs of the flock. ²⁹And Abimelech said to Abraham, "What is the meaning of these seven ewe lambs that you have set apart?" ³⁰He said, "These seven ewe lambs you shall accept from my hand, in order that you may

be a witness for me that I dug this well." ³¹Therefore that place was called Beer-sheba; because there both of them swore an oath. ³²When they had made a covenant at Beer-sheba, Abimelech, with Phicol the commander of his army, left and returned to the land of the Philistines. ³³Abraham planted a tamarisk tree in Beer-sheba, and called there on the name of the LORD, the Everlasting God. ³⁴And Abraham resided as an alien many days in the land of the Philistines.

After allowing this passage to speak to you, continue wrestling with the text through the teachings of the church and biblical scholarship.

Now that Abraham is assured of countless descendants through both Ishmael and Isaac, the narratives focus on Abraham's claim on the land. Abimelech, the king of Gerar, sees Abraham's growing prosperity and desires to establish a peaceful relationship with him. Abimelech wants to protect his family, his flocks, and most importantly, access to the wells of the desert. Abraham is shown with a new sense of confidence as his influence widens, and he is depicted here as a desert sheik on par with Abimelech. The king traveled from Gerar to Beer-sheba to speak with Abraham. Abimelech opened the dialogue by paying Abraham the highest compliment: "God is with you in all that you do" (v. 22).

Because Abraham was indeed prospering in every way, just as God had promised him upon leaving Haran, Abimelech wanted to enter a covenant with Abraham. The covenant would include a pact of mutual nonaggression, protecting their children and descendants through the generations (v. 23). Abimelech asked Abraham to swear he would not "deal falsely" with him or his posterity, probably alluding to the way Abraham had deceived him about Sarah (Gen. 20). The king also asked Abraham to deal loyally with him, as he had acted reliably with Abraham, recalling the way he had responded in settling the episode with Sarah. The covenant between Abimelech and Abraham takes the form of an oral oath, and the keeping of it is based on the two men's sense of honor and their belief that the divine witness to the pledge would punish the oath breaker. The covenant was solemnized as the two men slaughtered animals for a ritual sacrifice (v. 27).

As an example of this covenant between Abimelech and Abraham, the two men resolved an issue of disputed water rights. Abraham asserted his claim to a well that Abimelech's servants had seized, preventing Abraham from freely watering his herds. Abimelech responded by defending himself from blame, stating that his ignorance about the seizure had prevented him from correcting the matter.

Abraham presented Abimelech with seven ewe lambs in gratitude for the king's witness that Abraham had dug the well (vv. 28–30). By accepting them as a gift, Abimelech acknowledged Abraham's ownership of the well. Abraham named the place Beer-sheba, which means both "the well of seven" and "the well of the oath." The episode highlights the name Beer-sheba, since the Hebrew word *sheba*, meaning both "seven" and "swear an oath," is artfully woven into the entire passage. Beer-sheba would become the place most closely associated with Abraham.

After reading this encounter, write your responses to these questions:

‡ What was the purpose of the covenant between Abraham and Abimelech?

‡ In what ways are human relationships enhanced when God is the witness?

‡ In what ways does this human covenant reflect the divine covenant made by God with Abraham's descendants?

Meditatio

After reflecting on this passage, ask yourself how the text expands your relationship with God.

☩ What did the number "seven" mean for Abraham and Abimelech? Where else in the Bible does the number "seven" have special significance? Is the number significant in my life of faith?

☩ Abraham planted a tamarisk tree in Beer-sheba (v. 33). Why is the slow-growing, deep-rooted tree an effective memorial for the commitments involved in a covenant?

☩ The well of Abraham can still be seen today when visiting Beer-sheba. Why would a well be such an important possession in the time of Abraham? What might be an enduring memorial of my life someday?

Oratio

Remember that God cares about every aspect of your life and your relationships with others. Pray to God, who is always present and faithful to you.

El Olam, Everlasting God, you committed yourself to your people in the bond of the covenant, and you encourage us to make lasting commitments to others. Keep me faithful to my baptismal promises and to the other covenants I have made.

Continue praying to the Everlasting God in words that arise from the personal covenant God has formed with you . . .

Contemplatio

Trust in God's steadfast fidelity. Rest in the wonder of God's care for you while slowly repeating these words: "God is with you in all that you do" (v. 22).

Write a few words describing your contemplative experience of God's care.

Operatio

How has my life been shaped through God's covenant with me? What can I do to live more faithfully in covenant with my steadfast God?

15

Abraham's Supreme Test

Lectio

Read this text aloud so that you hear the words and listen to the inspired passage. As you read, underline or highlight the sections of the text that disturb you most.

GENESIS 22:1–8

¹After these things God tested Abraham. He said to him, "Abraham!" And he said, "Here I am." ²He said, "Take your son, your only son Isaac, whom you love, and go to the land of Moriah, and offer him there as a burnt offering on one of the mountains that I shall show you."

³So Abraham rose early in the morning, saddled his donkey, and took two of his young men with him, and his son Isaac; he cut the wood for the burnt offering, and set out and went to the place in the distance that God had shown him. ⁴On the third day Abraham looked up and saw the place far away. ⁵Then Abraham said to his young men, "Stay here with the donkey; the boy and I will go over there; we will worship, and then we will come back to you." ⁶Abraham took the wood of the burnt offering and laid it on his son Isaac, and he himself carried the fire and the knife. So the two of them walked on together. ⁷Isaac said to his father Abraham, "Father!" And he said, "Here I am, my son." He said, "The fire and the wood are here, but where is the lamb for a

burnt offering?" [8]Abraham said, "God himself will provide the lamb for a burnt offering, my son." So the two of them walked on together.

Continue listening for the Word of God in this Scripture passage as you explore its meaning through these comments.

We have arrived at the climactic episode of Abraham's long life, one of the Bible's most dramatic scenes. God's command to sacrifice Isaac is described as a "test" (v. 1), which is information imparted to the reader but not disclosed to Abraham. The Bible is filled with accounts of God's testing his people. This testing might seem unreasonable in light of our belief that God is all-knowing, but God is always engaged with his people—calling, leading, promising, providing, and yes, testing. God tests to determine who is serious about faith, to identify in whose lives he will fully be God, and to develop in his people certain desirable qualities for the life of faith. Like Job, Abraham is prepared to trust fully the God who gives and who takes away (Job 1:21).

God's first call to Abraham to leave Haran (12:1–4) and this last call to Abraham to go to Moriah are the two pillars that support the entire structure of Abraham's spiritual odyssey. The command of God is almost identical: "Go . . . to the land that I will show you" (12:1); "Go to the land of Moriah . . . on one of the mountains that I shall show you" (v. 2). In both calls, the enormity of what God asks is heightened by a series of increasingly painful terms with narrowing focus: "your country and your kindred and your father's house" (12:1); "your son, your only son Isaac, whom you love" (v. 2). In the first, Abraham is summoned to relinquish his entire past; in the second, he is called to give up his entire future, the promised son from whom Abraham would have countless descendants.

How does Abraham respond? Was he calm, angry, trusting, miserable, despairing? Did he pass a restless night before he "rose early in the morning" (v. 3)? We can only speculate about Abraham's emotions. His preparatory actions are described with a verbal scarcity appropriate to the solemn silence that pervades the scene: he rose, saddled, took, cut the wood, set out and went, looked up and saw. With only the sound of their sandals and the donkey's hooves in the desert sand, the long three-day trek allows time for somber reflection. Abraham could turn back at any time; his will was free; the burden of choice fell squarely on his shoulders. He knows that despite every reasonable impulse within him crying out to defy God's command, he must trustingly "go" once again, proving his faith and confirming his destiny. This is an epic journey.

Nearing the mountain of sacrifice, Abraham told his attendants to wait with the donkey while he and Isaac climb the road to the divinely chosen place. "We will worship, and then we will come back to you" (v. 5). Is Abraham simply trying to conceal from Isaac the true purpose of the journey, or does he harbor a secret hope that indeed they may both return? Abraham took the wood for the sacrifice and laid it on the shoulders of his son (v. 6). Isaac, unaware, carried the wood of his own destruction. "The two of them walked on together" (vv. 6–8)—Isaac in unsuspecting innocence and Abraham in unspeakable inner torment.

In the only words between the son and his father, Isaac asks, "The fire and the wood are here, but where is the lamb for a burnt offering?" (v. 7). Is this penetrating query simply an obvious question, or, in a culture in which child sacrifice was not unknown, is a suspicion of the dreadful truth beginning to dawn on Isaac? Abraham's trusting words, "God himself will provide the lamb for a burnt offering" (v. 8), expressed the hope that lay deep within him. Abraham knew that somehow the One who tested was also the One who provided.

After you have listened for the Word of the Lord, answer these questions:

✝ What are the similarities between the first call and the last call of Abraham?

✝ In what ways does the author heighten the drama of this account?

Meditatio

Read the episode again, engaging your full imagination. Pause to meditate each time a phrase speaks to you.

✝ What is most perplexing and shocking about this account for me? What are my unanswered questions?

✝ What did God really want from Abraham? How can testing help me to know myself better?

✝ What emotions might Abraham have experienced as he walked up the mountain with Isaac? What do I feel as I read this account?

Oratio

Use the images and emotions from your lectio and meditatio as the basis of your response to God. Pray to God with transparent confidence.

Father, I want to be able to entrust my life to you and to do what you ask of me. Give me the strength to always remain faithful to you and to trust your plan for my life.

Continue voicing the prayer that issues from your heart…

Contemplatio

Rest in the faith of Abraham. Imagine what it would be like to be totally confident in God's love and to trust God completely.

Write a few words about your experience of resting in Abraham's trusting faith.

Operatio

What have I learned about God through Abraham's supreme test? What practical impact could living in Abraham's faith make in my life?

16

The Binding of Isaac

Read the text aloud, attentively listening for the voice of God within the literary text.

GENESIS 22:9–19

⁹When they came to the place that God had shown him, Abraham built an altar there and laid the wood in order. He bound his son Isaac, and laid him on the altar, on top of the wood. ¹⁰Then Abraham reached out his hand and took the knife to kill his son. ¹¹But the angel of the LORD called to him from heaven, and said, "Abraham, Abraham!" And he said, "Here I am." ¹²He said, "Do not lay your hand on the boy or do anything to him; for now I know that you fear God, since you have not withheld your son, your only son, from me." ¹³And Abraham looked up and saw a ram, caught in a thicket by its horns. Abraham went and took the ram and offered it up as a burnt offering instead of his son. ¹⁴So Abraham called that place "The LORD will provide"; as it is said to this day, "On the mount of the LORD it shall be provided."

¹⁵The angel of the LORD called to Abraham a second time from heaven, ¹⁶and said, "By myself I have sworn, says the LORD: Because you have done this, and have not withheld your son, your only son, ¹⁷I will indeed bless you, and I will make your offspring as numerous

as the stars of heaven and as the sand that is on the seashore. And your offspring shall possess the gate of their enemies, [18]and by your offspring shall all the nations of the earth gain blessing for themselves, because you have obeyed my voice." [19]So Abraham returned to his young men, and they arose and went together to Beer-sheba; and Abraham lived at Beer-sheba.

After reading this narrative with your imagination and listening with your heart, continue to search for its meaning and significance for God's people.

The preparations for sacrifice are expressed in the starkest terms: Abraham built an altar, laid the wood upon it, bound his son, laid him on the altar, reached out his hand and took the knife (vv. 9–10). There is no dialogue; the anguished grief is beyond words. Is the knife the same instrument Abraham used to circumcise his infant son—an earlier expression of Abraham's trusting commitment to God? Since Abraham was elderly and Isaac was at least old enough to carry wood on his shoulder, surely the boy was strong enough to resist his father. But as Abraham was obedient to God, Isaac was obedient to his father and let himself be bound and placed on the altar.

At the moment Abraham raised his knife to slay his son, God's messenger called out to him and stayed his hand. "Now I know that you fear God, since you have not withheld your son, your only son, from me" (vv. 11–12). Abraham's commitment to God had been put to the ultimate test, and he had shown himself wholehearted in his self-surrender to God's will. It was not that God's foreknowledge of Abraham's character was lacking; rather, for Abraham's sake, his inner potential had to be demonstrated in action. Thereby, he became the exemplar of the God-fearing man, the model of genuine faith.

Abraham interprets the fortuitous presence of a ram to mean that God desires an animal sacrifice in place of his son (v. 13). We can't fully imagine the happiness as Isaac and Abraham watched the smoke of the offering ascend to God from the mountain that day. The use of the past tense of the same three verbs as in God's original order—go, take, and offer (v. 2)—indicate that in God's eyes Abraham accomplished what he had set out to do.

Abraham called the place "The LORD will provide" (v. 14), a reminder to all Abraham's descendants that God truly does provide for the needs of those who trust in him (v. 8). Abraham's greatest challenge proves that the God who tests is also the God who provides. Most of us only want a God who provides, but the life of Abraham teaches us that we cannot choose between these two baffling characteristics of God if we want to be people of faith.

Abraham's willingness to offer up his son to God (v. 16) helps us to better understand God's work in his Son Jesus. God asked Abraham to do what God would do in offering up his only beloved Son on the cross. "He who did not withhold his own Son, but gave him up for all of us" (Rom. 8:32) is the same God who tested and provided for Abraham. The obedient offering of Abraham strengthened God's covenant with Abraham. The one who had proven faithful would have descendants as numerous as the stars of heaven and the sand of the seashore, and all the nations of the earth would be blessed because Abraham obeyed God's voice (vv. 17–18).

Answer these questions after listening for the meaning of this sacred text:

✝ What is the most striking part of this episode for me?

✝ What is the most important offering Abraham made to God?

✝ In what way did Abraham's test strengthen his covenant with God and enable him to be an even greater blessing for all people?

Meditatio

Reflect on what is most surprising, instructive, and inspiring for you from the supreme test of Abraham.

‡ Mount Moriah (v. 2) was identified in later tradition with the temple mount in Jerusalem (2 Chron. 3:1). What does this connection with Abraham teach us about the sacrificial worship in the temple?

‡ What does Abraham demonstrate about his own character through the binding of Isaac? What has God taught me about myself through testing?

‡ In the New Testament, Paul writes, "God is faithful, and he will not let you be tested beyond your strength, but with the testing he will also provide the way out so that you may be able to endure it" (1 Cor. 10:13). How does Abraham's experience demonstrate the truth of Paul's words?

Oratio

Imagine the joyful gratitude expressed by Abraham and Isaac as the ram was sacrificed to God. Express your prayer after reflecting on this scene.

God of Abraham, you test your servants so that they may develop their faith and be identified as your own. Give me strength in times of testing and assure me that you will provide the way out.

Continue praying to God, using the words and images of the text to respond to God ...

Contemplatio

Remember that God not only tests but also provides. Trust in the God who provides for you and be grateful for God's loving care.

Write a few words summarizing your contemplative experience of God's tender protection.

Operatio

How did God shape the faith of Abraham through the binding of Isaac? How is God shaping my faith through this encounter with God's Word?

17

Abraham Purchases the Burial Cave at Hebron

Lectio

In a quiet and comfortable place, read the words of Scripture, seeking to understand their meaning.

GENESIS 23:1–16

¹Sarah lived one hundred twenty-seven years; this was the length of Sarah's life. ²And Sarah died at Kiriath-arba (that is, Hebron) in the land of Canaan; and Abraham went in to mourn for Sarah and to weep for her. ³Abraham rose up from beside his dead, and said to the Hittites, ⁴"I am a stranger and an alien residing among you; give me property among you for a burying place, so that I may bury my dead out of my sight." ⁵The Hittites answered Abraham, ⁶"Hear us, my lord; you are a mighty prince among us. Bury your dead in the choicest of our burial places; none of us will withhold from you any burial ground for burying your dead." ⁷Abraham rose and bowed to the Hittites, the people of the land. ⁸He said to them, "If you are willing that I should bury my dead out of my sight, hear me, and entreat for me Ephron son of Zohar, ⁹so that he may give me the cave of Machpelah, which he owns; it is at the end of his field. For the

full price let him give it to me in your presence as a possession for a burying place." [10]Now Ephron was sitting among the Hittites; and Ephron the Hittite answered Abraham in the hearing of the Hittites, of all who went in at the gate of his city, [11]"No, my lord, hear me; I give you the field, and I give you the cave that is in it; in the presence of my people I give it to you; bury your dead." [12]Then Abraham bowed down before the people of the land. [13]He said to Ephron in the hearing of the people of the land, "If you only will listen to me! I will give the price of the field; accept it from me, so that I may bury my dead there." [14]Ephron answered Abraham, [15]"My lord, listen to me; a piece of land worth four hundred shekels of silver—what is that between you and me? Bury your dead." [16]Abraham agreed with Ephron; and Abraham weighed out for Ephron the silver that he had named in the hearing of the Hittites, four hundred shekels of silver, according to the weights current among the merchants.

Search for the deeper meaning and significance of this inspired Scripture passage through this commentary.

There is wonderful freedom that comes with age: finally secure in our identity, less paralyzed by the opinions of others, free to say what we think and feel. Wouldn't it be wonderful if we could live life in reverse: born with lifelong wisdom, we would grow increasingly more youthful. But alas, we are destined to live with all the gains and losses of growing old. Abraham and Sarah are role models for older people. Their marriage had thrived through the crises of life: in midlife they took the risk to live their lives differently; they remained faithful through infertility, sexual jealousy, and family rivalry; they made sacrifices for each other and for their shared ideals; and most importantly, they left a legacy for future generations.

The span of Sarah's life confirms her great importance as Israel's first matriarch (v. 1). At her death, Abraham grieved for Sarah (v. 2). In the ancient world, mourning was never simply an interior emotion; it was also an external ritual. Abraham's mourning probably included wailing aloud, tearing his garments, cutting his beard, and putting on sackcloth for a set period of time. Though full of grief, Abraham had to see to the immediate practical need of finding a place for his wife's burial.

Because he was a resident alien, Abraham did not have an inherent right to buy land, and he was at a significant disadvantage in seeking a burial plot for Sarah. The scene offers us a fascinating glimpse into the subtleties of Middle Eastern negotiations. Land was looked upon as an ancestral trust, and there was a deep-seated fear that selling land to a foreigner would upset the social balance of the community. For this reason, it seems like the whole town of Hebron is involved in Abraham's transaction. Through courteous give and take, bestowing polite titles and profound bows, a permanent burial cave is secured for the family of Abraham.

Abraham met the elders of Hebron at the city gates, where all official business was conducted. Identifying himself as a foreigner among the Hittites, he acknowledged that he was at their mercy. Because of Abraham's high status among the local townspeople, they first offered him the choicest burial place of the community (v. 6). But Abraham knew exactly which piece of property he wanted. It was the cave of Machpelah, located at the end of a field owned by Ephron son of Zohar (vv. 8–9). Abraham wanted to own the property in perpetuity and was willing to do whatever was necessary to secure his ownership. To ensure that his descendants' claim to the property would not be contested in the future, Abraham insisted on paying a full price and on conducting the negotiations in full view of the citizens. When Ephron, with seeming nonchalance, offered to sell the entire field to Abraham for four hundred shekels of silver, Abraham immediately accepted his opening offer and weighed out the exact amount (vv. 10–16). Abraham knew that, in the matter of his family's burial cave, a binding contract was more important than a good price.

After carefully reading the Scripture and commentary, answer these questions:

✝ What was involved in the external rituals of grief and mourning in the time of the patriarchs and matriarchs?

Meditatio

Spend some time reflecting on the text, asking yourself what personal message the passage has for you.

✧ What are the qualities that make Abraham and Sarah models for a healthy and lasting marriage? What of their example can I imitate?

✧ Could there be a link between monotheism (belief in one God) and monogamy (commitment to one spouse)? How does monotheism affect my commitments?

✧ Have I thought about making arrangements for my funeral? How would I hope to be eulogized?

Oratio

Using the ideas generated by the text, spend some time responding to God with words that flow from your reflection.

> God of the living and the dead, you want me to live my life in such a way that it becomes an example for the next generation. Keep me faithful and devoted to those I love so that my life might reflect the loyalty of your covenant with me.

Continue responding to God with words generated by your reflection on the Scripture . . .

Contemplatio

In silent stillness, as if you were at the entrance of the cave of Machpelah, receptively allow God to fill you with his divine presence.

Write a brief note about your experience of contemplation, gazing into the stillness of the cave.

Operatio

What have I learned about myself through this lectio divina today? How is God shaping my life through my reflective reading of this passage?

18

Burial of Sarah
and Abraham

Lectio

Kiss the words of Scripture, asking God to help you reverence the divine Word within. Be grateful for God's invitation to listen to Scripture.

GENESIS 23:17–20; 25:7–11

[17]So the field of Ephron in Machpelah, which was to the east of Mamre, the field with the cave that was in it and all the trees that were in the field, throughout its whole area, passed [18]to Abraham as a possession in the presence of the Hittites, in the presence of all who went in at the gate of his city. [19]After this, Abraham buried Sarah his wife in the cave of the field of Machpelah facing Mamre (that is, Hebron) in the land of Canaan. [20]The field and the cave that is in it passed from the Hittites into Abraham's possession as a burying place.

[7]This is the length of Abraham's life, one hundred seventy-five years. [8]Abraham breathed his last and died in a good old age, an old man and full of years, and was gathered to his people. [9]His sons Isaac and Ishmael buried him in the cave of Machpelah, in the field of Ephron son of Zohar the Hittite, east of Mamre, [10]the field that

Abraham purchased from the Hittites. There Abraham was buried, with his wife Sarah. ¹¹After the death of Abraham God blessed his son Isaac. And Isaac settled at Beer-lahai-roi.

After carefully reading these final texts of Abraham's life, consider their meaning in light of God's saving revelation.

The cave of Machpelah in Hebron is the first piece of real estate in the Promised Land secured by the patriarch. Its purchase is confirmed in legal detail: identity of the transferor, location of the property, description of its contents, identity of the purchaser, and affirmation of official witnesses (23:17–18). Though it is a small piece of real estate, a single field with its trees and a cave, the importance of this site is monumental for the future of Abraham's descendants.

By choosing to be buried in Canaan, rather than back in the land of their births, Abraham and Sarah put down roots in the soil that God had promised to their descendants. The cave of Machpelah is the first foothold of a vast inheritance for future generations. According to Genesis, not only Abraham and Sarah are buried there but also Isaac and his wife Rebekah, and their son Jacob and his wife Leah. Throughout the biblical period, the cave was an important shrine and a symbol of Israelite unity.

Today the cave of Machpelah in Hebron is revered by Jews, Muslims, and Christians, since all the children of Abraham pay their respects to the great patriarchs and matriarchs. The Arab people identify the site as Haram el-Khalil, "the sacred precinct of the friend of God." The Jewish people consider it their most sacred monument after the Western Wall in Jerusalem. The surrounding wall of huge stones that stands today goes back to the time of Herod. Later in the Byzantine period, a church was built over the site, and with the Arab conquest in the seventh century, the church was converted into a mosque. Sadly, no place on earth, except for the temple mount in Jerusalem, has been the object of more violent struggle among Abraham's descendants.

After the burial of Sarah, Abraham lived another thirty-eight years. During those years, Abraham found a worthy bride for his son Isaac, as it was the custom of the time for parents to arrange their children's marriages

(Gen. 24). Abraham also married again, taking a wife named Keturah, with whom he had several more children who would also father nations (25:1–4). Though Isaac received his inheritance, Abraham provided for all of his children in his last years (25:5–6).

Abraham, like Sarah, lived a long and blessed life (25:7–8). After he exhaled the air of this world for the last time, both of his sons, Isaac and Ishmael, came together to bury their father, a task that transcended their rivalry (25:9). Both sons were loved by their father; both were promised abundant blessings; both would be fathers of nations. While the biblical story continues with Isaac and his family, Genesis does not fail to note the twelve sons of Ishmael (25:12–16), the descendants of whom were the Arab people (25:18). Many centuries later, some of the Arab people became the first disciples of the Abrahamic faith that came to be called Islam. If there is ever to be peace between the offspring of Ishmael and Isaac, they must offer one another a reconciliation as profound as the moment when the two brothers came together to bury their father Abraham.

After hearing the words of this text, try to answer the following questions:

‡ Why is it significant that Abraham and Sarah chose to be buried in the land of Canaan?

‡ What brought the two sons of Abraham together after decades of estrangement?

‡ Why is the cave of Machpelah a place of strife as well as a symbol of hope?

Meditatio

Spend some time meditating on the life of Abraham as expressed in the texts of Genesis that you have read.

✝ What does the legacy of Abraham teach me about God? In what way has my understanding of Abraham's spiritual paternity grown stronger after reflecting on these inspired texts?

✝ Why did Ishmael and Isaac come together to bury their father? What does this encounter teach me about forgiveness and reconciliation between individuals and among the peoples of the world?

✝ What parallels do I see between my journey of faith and that of Abraham?

Oratio

Pray to God from your heart in whatever way responds to the divine Word spoken to you through this text of Genesis.

God of our ancestors, from age to age you have gathered your people to yourself in death. May I remember those who have gone before me, my physical and spiritual ancestors, and trust that you will unite me with them where we will praise you forever.

Continue praying using the biblical vocabulary you have heard . . .

Contemplatio

Imagine you are in the silence of the cave with Ishmael and Isaac. Let the power of healing grief and forgiveness work within your heart.

Write a few words from your contemplation within the cave.

Operatio

What forgiveness and reconciliation need to happen in my heart today? What practical challenges do the Scriptures of Genesis present for me?

19

The Promises God Made to Abraham

In your quiet space, light a candle and set it in front of you as you read. Vocalize the words of the text so that you not only read with your eyes but hear with your ears.

EXODUS 3:1–6, 13–16; 6:2–9

¹Moses was keeping the flock of his father-in-law Jethro, the priest of Midian; he led his flock beyond the wilderness, and came to Horeb, the mountain of God. ²There the angel of the LORD appeared to him in a flame of fire out of a bush; he looked, and the bush was blazing, yet it was not consumed. ³Then Moses said, "I must turn aside and look at this great sight, and see why the bush is not burned up." ⁴When the LORD saw that he had turned aside to see, God called to him out of the bush, "Moses, Moses!" And he said, "Here I am." ⁵Then he said, "Come no closer! Remove the sandals from your feet, for the place on which you are standing is holy ground." ⁶He said further, "I am the God of your father, the God of Abraham, the God of Isaac, and the God of Jacob." And Moses hid his face, for he was afraid to look at God.

¹³But Moses said to God, "If I come to the Israelites and say to them, 'The God of your ancestors has sent me to you,' and they

ask me, 'What is his name?' what shall I say to them?" [14]God said to Moses, "I AM WHO I AM." He said further, "Thus you shall say to the Israelites, 'I AM has sent me to you.'" [15]God also said to Moses, "Thus you shall say to the Israelites, 'The LORD, the God of your ancestors, the God of Abraham, the God of Isaac, and the God of Jacob, has sent me to you':

This is my name forever,
and this my title for all generations.

[16]Go and assemble the elders of Israel, and say to them, 'The LORD, the God of your ancestors, the God of Abraham, of Isaac, and of Jacob, has appeared to me, saying: I have given heed to you and to what has been done to you in Egypt.'"

[2]God also spoke to Moses and said to him: "I am the LORD. [3]I appeared to Abraham, Isaac, and Jacob as God Almighty, but by my name 'The LORD' I did not make myself known to them. [4]I also established my covenant with them, to give them the land of Canaan, the land in which they resided as aliens. [5]I have also heard the groaning of the Israelites whom the Egyptians are holding as slaves, and I have remembered my covenant. [6]Say therefore to the Israelites, 'I am the LORD, and I will free you from the burdens of the Egyptians and deliver you from slavery to them. I will redeem you with an outstretched arm and with mighty acts of judgment. [7]I will take you as my people, and I will be your God. You shall know that I am the LORD your God, who has freed you from the burdens of the Egyptians. [8]I will bring you into the land that I swore to give to Abraham, Isaac, and Jacob; I will give it to you for a possession. I am the LORD.'" [9]Moses told this to the Israelites; but they would not listen to Moses, because of their broken spirit and their cruel slavery.

After pondering these ancient texts, turn to this commentary to seek richer and fuller meaning in the inspired Scripture.

Many centuries after the life of Abraham, his descendants were living in the land of Egypt. The sons of Jacob, Abraham's great-grandsons, had gone to Egypt to escape from a famine in the land of Canaan. They continued to live there for many generations, and eventually they were made slaves of the Egyptians, being used as manual labor for the many building projects of the pharaoh.

In offering Abraham a glimpse into the distant future, God had told him, "Know this for certain, that your offspring shall be aliens in a land that is not theirs, and shall be slaves there, and they shall be oppressed for four hundred years; but I will bring judgment on the nation that they serve, and afterward they shall come out with great possessions" (Gen. 15:13–14). Having promised release from their bondage, God began to execute the exodus of Abraham's offspring from the slavery of Egypt by calling a man named Moses.

When God called to Moses from the midst of the blazing bush, he identified himself in a way that Moses would recognize: "I am the God of your father, the God of Abraham, the God of Isaac, and the God of Jacob (3:6; see 3:15–16). This is the same God who had identified himself to Abraham as God Almighty (*El Shaddai*, in Hebrew) and had entered into covenant with him (6:3; Gen. 17:1–2). As Abraham had come to realize, this one God could not be localized in an idol, or controlled by ritual, or captured in a name. "I AM WHO I AM" (3:14) could only be known through his dynamic action in the lives of his people.

Just as God had rescued Sarah and Abraham long ago in Egypt by inflicting "plagues" on Pharaoh (Gen. 12:17) and as God had heard the cry of Hagar and Ishmael in their distress and had come to their rescue (Gen. 21:17), God has now heard the cry of the Hebrew people in Egypt and will come to release them from their bondage (6:5–6). God's covenant with Abraham is the all-important link with God from the past (6:3–4). God's promises given to Abraham long ago are now being actualized in God's liberating action on behalf of his struggling people.

The freedom God wants for his people is not just a liberation from oppression; it is also the freedom to live in a land of blessing. The land God had promised to Abraham and his posterity is the land to which God would bring Moses and his people. God said to Moses, "I will bring you into the land that I swore to give to Abraham, Isaac, and Jacob; I will give it to you for a possession" (6:8). The children of Abraham were coming back to the land of promise.

Meditatio

Use your imagination to enter the scene of the desert, the mountain, and the fire. Read the passage again slowly. Repeat and ponder whatever words or phrases strike you from your reading.

‡ By what names does God identify himself to Moses? What do these names tell me about the nature of God?

‡ What is conveyed by God's identification of himself as "the God of Abraham"? What heritage and faith have I received from my ancestors?

‡ What personal message is God offering me in this scene? How reluctant am I to respond to God's call? What would it take to respond to him with an obedient heart?

Oratio

Hear God speaking to you: "Remove the sandals from your feet, for the place on which you are standing is holy ground" (3:5). Take off your shoes and pray to God.

> Lord God Almighty, you answer your people when they cry out to you, and you rescue the oppressed with your mighty hand. You are faithful through generation after generation. Help me to trust in you.

Continue praying to the One who knows you intimately, cares about you deeply, and accepts you unconditionally . . .

Contemplatio

Imagine you are in the silence and stillness of the desert. Just sit shoeless in the presence of God and place yourself under his loving gaze. Repeat the sacred name of God, "I AM WHO I AM," (3:5) to keep your mind focused. Enjoy these holy moments for as long as you wish.

Write a few words from your silent contemplation before the living God.

Operatio

After his encounter with God, Moses returned to his people and became God's liberating instrument. What is God calling me to do through his inspired Word? Why am I reluctant to hear God's invitation?

20

Song of Abraham's Offspring

This song of praise and thanksgiving has been prayed by Israelites and Christians for thousands of years. Slowly articulate the words of the psalm or chant them joyfully. Hear the voices of the generations before you who have sung this psalm and join in their praise.

PSALM 105:1–11

¹O give thanks to the LORD, call on his name,
  make known his deeds among the peoples.
²Sing to him, sing praises to him;
  tell of all his wonderful works.
³Glory in his holy name;
  let the hearts of those who seek the LORD rejoice.
⁴Seek the LORD and his strength;
  seek his presence continually.
⁵Remember the wonderful works he has done,
  his miracles, and the judgments he uttered,
⁶O offspring of his servant Abraham,
  children of Jacob, his chosen ones.

⁷He is the Lord our God;
  his judgments are in all the earth.
⁸He is mindful of his covenant forever,
  of the word that he commanded, for a thousand generations,
⁹the covenant that he made with Abraham,
  his sworn promise to Isaac,
¹⁰which he confirmed to Jacob as a statute,
  to Israel as an everlasting covenant,
¹¹saying, "To you I will give the land of Canaan
  as your portion for an inheritance."

After experiencing this psalm through its descriptive images and joyful praise, continue seeking its timeless significance.

In the Psalms, the people of Israel express their faith through poetic song. Sung in the liturgies of Jerusalem's temple and in the communal celebrations of Israel's people, the Psalms convey the beliefs and emotions of the people of God. This psalm is a hymn of praise for God's trustworthiness and fidelity to the covenant.

Those addressed by the psalm are the "offspring of his servant Abraham" (v. 6). A series of imperatives calls the congregation to give thanks to the Lord, call on his name, make known his deeds, sing praises to him, glory in his holy name, seek him, and remember his wonderful works (vv. 1–5).

In forty-five verses, the psalm recounts the primary historical deeds of God at work in the history of his people, from the covenant with Abraham through the exodus from Egypt and entry into the Promised Land. The entire series of wondrous events is the result of God's remembering the covenant with Abraham: "For he remembered his holy promise, and Abraham, his servant" (v. 42).

Abraham is called God's "servant" (vv. 6, 42). In Israel's culture, a servant was a person who belonged to another and who lived in the context of that belonging. The servant's identity was determined by the one he served. In turn, the servant was protected and supported by the person to whom the servant belonged. Thus the transfer was fairly easy from the concept of human servant to that of God's servant. In the Bible, those who give special service to God receive the title of servant of God: first Abraham, then Moses, Joshua, prophets, kings, Israel, and the Messiah.

The primary theme of "covenant" (vv. 8–11) stresses that the foundational events of salvation are God's initiative. He is the exclusive actor in the long list of wonderful works. God orchestrates everything for his people's benefit. The covenant is also called "the word," "sworn promise," and "statute." God's remembering the covenant has guided all God's actions in bringing his people into the land. The covenant is "everlasting." God will be mindful of his covenant "forever," "for a thousand generations" (v. 8). What God initiated in Abraham has only just begun.

After praying these words with the generations before you, try to respond to these questions:

‡ What indicates that this psalm was sung in communal worship of God?

‡ What words of the psalm indicate the mood in which it was sung?

‡ Which aspects of God's covenant are highlighted in this psalm?

Meditatio

Make the prayer of the psalmist your own prayer. Let it interact with your own praise, thanks, and rejoicing.

✝ What is the value of periodically "remembering" God's wonderful works? What are some of God's wonders I should remember?

✝ What does it mean to be a servant of God? What are the implications for my life?

✝ In what way are the events in my life's history the result of God's initiative?

Oratio

Pray the psalm again from your own heart. Add your own words. Praise God for his wondrous deeds and the promises of his everlasting covenant.

> Lord God, in every age you remember the promises you made to Abraham. I thank you for the heritage of faith you have given me and for the blessings you have bestowed upon me. May I give you thanks, sing your praise, and make known your deeds.

Continue pouring out your prayer to God until words are no longer necessary or useful . . .

Contemplatio

Heed the words of the psalm: "Seek the LORD and his strength; seek his presence continually." (v. 4). In praise of God beyond what words can express, rest in the silence of God's loving embrace and trust in him.

Write a few words about your experience of seeking God's presence.

Operatio

Choose a phrase from the psalm to memorize. Learn it by heart and take it with you as you leave your time of prayer. Repeat it often as you go about your day or night.

21

The Rock from Which We Were Hewn

Lectio

Listen to these voices from the past to hear how our spiritual ancestors re-membered the lives of Abraham and Sarah. Pay attention to the ways they exhort people of every age to gain strength in present challenges.

ISAIAH 51:1–2

¹Listen to me, you that pursue righteousness,
   you that seek the LORD.
Look to the rock from which you were hewn,
   and to the quarry from which you were dug.
²Look to Abraham your father
   and to Sarah who bore you;
for he was but one when I called him,
   but I blessed him and made him many.

SIRACH 44:19–21

¹⁹Abraham was the great father of a multitude of nations,
   And no one has been found like him in glory.
²⁰He kept the law of the Most High,
   and entered into a covenant with him;

he certified the covenant with his flesh,
    and when he was tested he proved faithful.
²¹Therefore the Lord assured him with an oath
    that the nations would be blessed through his offspring;
    that he would make him as numerous as the dust of the earth,
    and exalt his offspring like the stars,
    and give them an inheritance from sea to sea
    and from the Euphrates to the ends of the earth.

Reflect on these poetic texts in order to understand the outlook of your ancestors and make it your own.

This passage from the prophet Isaiah was written during the exile of the Jewish people in Babylon (sixth century BC). Though the exiles have remained faithful to God, they are discouraged and disheartened by their captivity and seeming powerlessness. They fear that, even if they are able to return to Judah, they will not be able to face the overwhelming task of restoring their homeland because they are so weak and few in number. Isaiah offers these exiles an encouraging message, calling them to look back to the example of their ancestors, Abraham and Sarah.

Though these exiles lived well over a thousand years after the lives of Abraham and Sarah, the prophet still holds up these ancestors as the inspiring model for their descendants to imitate. The metaphors of "rock" and "quarry" (Isa. 51:1) refer to the solid conviction and foundational source of faith offered by Israel's patriarch and matriarch.

Though Abraham was elderly and childless when he was called, God "blessed him and made him many" (Isa. 51:2). Based on God's assurances to Abraham, the exiles can be confident that God will bless them with strength and abundance as they prepare to make the same journey as Abraham, returning to their home in the Promised Land. The promises made to Abraham continue to be fulfilled in every age.

The book of Sirach was written by a Jewish teacher in Jerusalem (second century BC) who wanted to instill within his young students a loving respect for the traditions of their ancestors. Sirach wanted to help his students find a balance between living in the contemporary world and respecting the faith of their ancestors. The final chapters of his work consist of a poetic hymn of praise to the heroes of Israel's past, seeking to motivate his young hearers to similar loyalty.

Sirach refers to Abraham as "the great father of a multitude of nations" (Sir. 44:19). He then lists four of Abraham's outstanding merits: he kept God's law, he made a covenant with God, he certified the covenant through circumcision, and he proved faithful when he was tested (Sir. 44:20). In response, God assured Abraham of three promises: the nations would be blessed through his offspring, his progeny would be as numerous as the dust of the earth and as exalted as the stars, and his posterity would receive a vast inheritance (Sir. 44:21). "Sea to sea" and "to the ends of the earth" express an idealistic expanse and the universal breadth of Abraham's blessings.

After hearing these voices of the past, answer these questions:

✝ What were the challenges that faced the first hearers of Isaiah's words?

✝ What did Sirach wish to do for his young listeners?

✝ Why is it so challenging to live in the contemporary world while respecting the faith of one's ancestors?

Meditatio

Reflect on the words of these texts as if they were spoken to you. Allow the words of encouragement to lift you up.

✝ In what areas of my life do I feel discouraged and powerless? What word of hope do these Scriptures offer to me?

✝ Why are the terms "rock" and "quarry" effective metaphors for describing the role of our biblical ancestors?

✝ In what way could Abraham be a model and inspiration for young people today? What qualities does he inspire in the young?

Oratio

Respond to God's Word to you with your own words to God. Speak from your heart in response to the hope you have been offered.

Most High God, you called our ancestors to a committed life in covenant with you. Help me to learn from their example and be inspired by their heroism so that I may leave a legacy to the generations after me.

Continue to express your hopes, desires, struggles, and commitment...

Contemplatio

In silent stillness, place yourself under the loving gaze of God and allow God to fill your heart with his divine presence. Entrust your future to God.

Write a few words about the confidence and conviction that fills your heart.

Operatio

Exhorted by God's Word, what new hope and renewed sense of mission have I received? How will my life be different today after encountering God through these Scriptures?

22.

Descendants of Abraham through Faith

Lectio

When the Genesis texts of Abraham are read in the light of Jesus Christ, we see their fuller meaning in God's ultimate plan. Read Paul's letter to understand how the life of Abraham laid the foundation for life in Christ.

GALATIANS 3:6–9, 15–18

⁶Just as Abraham "believed God, and it was reckoned to him as righteousness," ⁷so, you see, those who believe are the descendants of Abraham. ⁸And the scripture, foreseeing that God would justify the Gentiles by faith, declared the gospel beforehand to Abraham, saying, "All the Gentiles shall be blessed in you." ⁹For this reason, those who believe are blessed with Abraham who believed.

¹⁵Brothers and sisters, I give an example from daily life: once a person's will has been ratified, no one adds to it or annuls it. ¹⁶Now the promises were made to Abraham and to his offspring; it does not say, "And to offsprings," as of many; but it says, "And to your offspring," that is, to one person, who is Christ. ¹⁷My point is this: the law, which came four hundred thirty years later, does not annul a covenant previously ratified by God, so as to nullify the promise.

¹⁸For if the inheritance comes from the law, it no longer comes from the promise; but God granted it to Abraham through the promise.

Continue seeking the meaning and significance of Paul's words for you and for Christ's church.

Jesus was a Jew, a "son of Abraham," as the opening verse of the New Testament declares (Matt. 1:1). All the major figures in the life of Jesus and the early church were from the people of Israel, and the church began as a sect of Judaism. Paul himself was proud of his Jewish heritage, as he frequently testified in his letters: "I myself am an Israelite, a descendant of Abraham" (Rom. 11:1). When Paul began his missionary travels, he always preached first in the synagogue of each town he visited. Though Jesus had certainly opened a new era in the history of God's relationship with his chosen people, for Paul that newness was in continuity with God's actions in Israel's history.

Paul's letter to the Galatians focuses on the issues that arose as non-Jews (Gentiles) began to accept the Good News of Jesus Christ. Paul was convinced that the gospel by its very nature was directed to Gentiles as well as to Jews, but he was equally convinced that Jesus was the fulfillment of Jewish expectations rooted in the promises contained in the ancient Scriptures. The fundamental questions, then, are the following: In light of the coming of Christ, who makes up the people of God? What is the distinguishing characteristic of God's people? Who, in fact, are "descendants of Abraham"?

Paul responds to these questions by quoting from the accounts of Abraham in Genesis. First, he quotes Genesis 15:6, which states: Abraham "believed the LORD; and the LORD reckoned it to him as righteousness." Paul explains that Abraham's belief in God was the characteristic that brought about his right relationship with God. Therefore, Abraham's true descendants must be those who "believe," those who relate to God through faith (vv. 6–7). This means that, for Paul, the distinctive characteristic of being the people of God is faith, not biological descent or following the law given to Moses.

Paul's second quotation is from Genesis 12:3, which states: In Abraham, "all the families of the earth shall be blessed." Paul acclaims this verse as a foreshadowing of the Good News, "the gospel beforehand" (v. 8). This message of Good News implies that at some future time all the nations (Gentiles as well as Jews) will be blessed as heirs of Abraham. For Paul, Christ is the fulfillment of this hope. His salvation is offered to all people who accept God's grace in faith. The movement of the gospel of Jesus Christ outward to the Gentiles is not just Paul's way of extending the mission; it was God's plan since the call of Abraham.

The truest "offspring" of Abraham is Christ (v. 16). His life redefined the people of God and opened the door to the whole world. Paul points out that the "promise" given to Abraham preceded the "law" given to Moses by four hundred and thirty years (vv. 17–18). Since the covenant with Moses cannot negate the covenant with Abraham, entry into the people of God is through believing in the promise, not just obeying the law. The sole criteria for sharing in God's blessings is faith in Christ, not following the prescripts of the law.

After carefully reading Paul's text and the commentary, answer these questions about your reading:

‡ What characteristic of Abraham does Paul urge his readers to imitate?

‡ What aspects of God's covenant with Abraham are emphasized in Paul's letter?

Meditatio

✝ Why does Paul describe Genesis 12:3 as "the gospel beforehand"? In what way is this verse a foreshadowing of the Good News of Christ during the time of Abraham?

✝ In what way does Paul broaden the Jewish understanding of "descendants of Abraham" (v. 7)? In what way am I a descendant of Abraham?

✝ What aspects of the gospel of Jesus Christ convince me that it is destined for all people, not just for its first Jewish followers?

Oratio

Resolve today to deepen your trust in God as you seek to imitate the faith of Abraham. Offer your prayer to God in these words or your own words.

> Lord God, your promises extend from Abraham to all the people of the world. Help me to receive your promises with trusting confidence so that I may truly be a descendant of Abraham and a member of your people.

Continue to express your prayer to God with a heart full of faith . . .

Contemplatio

Be still, knowing that you have inherited the promises of God. Let your heart be filled with gratitude for the inheritance you have received.

Write a few words about the gratitude you feel.

Operatio

What difference does it make if I consider myself an heir to God's covenant with Abraham? What outlook or actions arise from this inheritance I have received?

23

Our Example of Faith

As you study this text and commentary, highlight or underline the parts you wish to remember and return to for reflection. Let the Holy Spirit guide your careful reading.

ROMANS 4:1–12

¹What then are we to say was gained by Abraham, our ancestor according to the flesh? ²For if Abraham was justified by works, he has something to boast about, but not before God. ³For what does the scripture say? "Abraham believed God, and it was reckoned to him as righteousness." ⁴Now to one who works, wages are not reckoned as a gift but as something due. ⁵But to one who without works trusts him who justifies the ungodly, such faith is reckoned as righteousness. ⁶So also David speaks of the blessedness of those to whom God reckons righteousness apart from works:

⁷"Blessed are those whose iniquities are forgiven,
    and whose sins are covered;
⁸blessed is the one against whom the LORD will not reckon sin."

⁹Is this blessedness, then, pronounced only on the circumcised, or also on the uncircumcised? We say, "Faith was reckoned to Abraham

as righteousness." [10]How then was it reckoned to him? Was it before or after he had been circumcised? It was not after, but before he was circumcised. [11]He received the sign of circumcision as a seal of the righteousness that he had by faith while he was still uncircumcised. The purpose was to make him the ancestor of all who believe without being circumcised and who thus have righteousness reckoned to them, [12]and likewise the ancestor of the circumcised who are not only circumcised but who also follow the example of the faith that our ancestor Abraham had before he was circumcised.

After you have heard these inspired words of Paul with your heart, continue to explore their significance for the life of discipleship.

The figure of Abraham is more prominent in Paul's writings than any other individual except for Jesus. Here Paul invokes Abraham as his exemplar to verify the proposal he set forth in Romans 3:28: "For we hold that a person is justified by faith apart from works prescribed by the law." In order to demonstrate this truth, Paul refers to the life of Abraham as recorded in Genesis. Abraham continually believed in God's promises of a son and the blessings that would ensue despite overwhelming evidence to the contrary. He trusted God's covenant in spite of seemingly insurmountable obstacles: Sarah's barrenness, his own old age, the rejection of Ishmael, and decades of waiting. Abraham's own resources were exhausted; there was nothing Abraham could do. The only choice was humble submission and confident trust. Thus, "Abraham believed God" (v. 3), personally and completely.

Abraham's achievements were utterly extraordinary. He left the civilization of Ur to travel to an unknown land, he carved out a life for Sarah and himself in the nomadic wilderness of Canaan, he fought battles with desert kings, he interceded for Sodom before God, and he demonstrated a willingness to sacrifice even his beloved son. If anyone had a reason to boast, it would be Abraham (v. 2). But despite the praiseworthiness of these deeds, they were of no consequence in realizing God's promises. Abraham simply trusted in the credibility of God. He was not justified by his works but by his faith.

God's promises to Abraham were not a reward for Abraham's obedience and good performance, for God called Abraham and promised him blessings and progeny before he had responded in obedience (Gen. 12:1–3). It was

Abraham's faith in God that justified him: "Abraham believed God, and it was reckoned to him as righteousness" (v. 3). God regarded Abraham as righteous (Gen. 15:6) before Abraham had been either tested (Gen. 22) or circumcised (Gen. 17). His blessings were not given by God as a reward for something good he had done, like wages given to a worker (v. 4). Righteousness was not Abraham's due; it was God's gift, the act of God's gracious will.

Abraham is the bearer of God's promised blessings to all people. Because he is our father in faith, when we share in his faith we become his descendants. For Paul and other Jews, Abraham is their "ancestor according to the flesh" (v. 1). But for everyone else, Abraham is the "ancestor of all who believe" (v. 11). We become descendants of Abraham by sharing his faithful trust, not his genes.

Paul's Jewish contemporaries believed that God justifies those within the covenant, while the "ungodly" stand outside the covenant. But Paul taught that God justifies the "ungodly" (v. 5) through their faith and bestows blessings on both the circumcised and the uncircumcised (vv. 9–12). If God justified Abraham before he was circumcised, then he was not a Jew at the time of his justification. Abraham was an uncircumcised Gentile when he was reckoned righteous by God. Thus Abraham was the father of Gentile believers before he was the father of Jewish believers. His becoming forefather of the Jewish people followed his fatherhood of all believers.

For Paul and the early Christian church, this meant that both Gentile and Jewish followers of Jesus could appeal to Abraham as father. Both groups are included within Abraham's fatherhood of faith, and neither is pitted against the other. There is not one way to salvation for Jews and another for Gentiles. Through Abraham we know that trusting faith in God is not a new means to salvation, supplanting the keeping of the law, but rather the oldest and truest means.

After studying this text, review your understanding with this question:

✝ How is Abraham the father not only of Jews but of all believers?

Meditatio

Spend some time reflecting on those verses and sentences you highlighted during your lectio. Use your insights to respond to the following questions:

‡ What parts of Abraham's life are most extraordinary and praiseworthy for me? Why does Abraham not boast in his accomplishments?

‡ Does it matter to me whether a right relationship with God is a gift to be received or a reward to be earned? What difference does it make to me practically and emotionally?

‡ What are the global implications of the fact that Abraham is the father of all believers?

Oratio

All believers are one family because of the faith of Abraham. Pray for the gift of faith both for yourself and for the people of our world.

God of our ancestors, through the cross of Jesus Christ you extended the blessings promised to Abraham to the whole world. Help me realize that I cannot earn your salvation but that I can only accept the gift of your saving grace through a living faith in Christ.

Continue this prayer in words that issue from your heart . . .

Contemplatio

When words are no longer helpful, just rest in God's presence with trusting confidence. Realize that God is transforming you from within through the gift of faith that now fills your heart.

Write a few words about your contemplative experience.

Operatio

Paul's heart was filled with zeal and dedication to his evangelizing mission. How do Paul's words inspire me with a desire to evangelize and share my faith with those around me? How can I best show others the impact of my faith today?

24

God's Promises Inherited through Faith

Lectio

Put away the distractions of the day and enter a quiet place where you can hear God's voice speaking to you through the words of Scripture. Ask the Holy Spirit to teach you about God's promises as you read.

ROMANS 4:13–25

[13]For the promise that he would inherit the world did not come to Abraham or to his descendants through the law but through the righteousness of faith. [14]If it is the adherents of the law who are to be the heirs, faith is null and the promise is void. [15]For the law brings wrath; but where there is no law, neither is there violation.

[16]For this reason it depends on faith, in order that the promise may rest on grace and be guaranteed to all his descendants, not only to the adherents of the law but also to those who share the faith of Abraham (for he is the father of all of us, [17]as it is written, "I have made you the father of many nations")—in the presence of the God in whom he believed, who gives life to the dead and calls into existence the things that do not exist. [18]Hoping against hope, he believed that he would become "the father of many nations," according to what was said, "So

numerous shall your descendants be." [19]He did not weaken in faith when he considered his own body, which was already as good as dead (for he was about a hundred years old), or when he considered the barrenness of Sarah's womb. [20]No distrust made him waver concerning the promise of God, but he grew strong in his faith as he gave glory to God, [21]being fully convinced that God was able to do what he had promised. [22]Therefore his faith "was reckoned to him as righteousness."

[23]Now the words, "it was reckoned to him," were written not for his sake alone, [24]but for ours also. It will be reckoned to us who believe in him who raised Jesus our Lord from the dead, [25]who was handed over to death for our trespasses and was raised for our justification.

Continue listening for God's Word as you seek the fullest meaning of this Scripture passage through this commentary.

Paul refers to God's promise that Abraham would "inherit the world" (v. 13). That promise, given to Abraham nearly two millennia before Paul, would not remain the possession of only one segment of humanity. Like yeast in the dough, Abraham's descendants would grow to permeate the whole world. His offspring would surpass the bounds of Israel and include the Gentiles so that God's salvation would be offered to everyone. His heirs would be all people who walk by faith. He is the "father of many nations"; he is the "father of us all" (vv. 16–18).

The God in whom Abraham believed is the God "who gives life to the dead and calls into existence the things that do not exist" (v. 17). Abraham experienced these manifestations of the God of life. The bodies of Abraham and Sarah were dead to the possibility of producing an heir. At the moment when their beloved son was doomed to die in sacrifice, God restored him to life. The creating and redeeming God of Abraham brought an inheritance into being in a way that seemed totally impossible.

The only response to such a God is faith. Trying to earn the favor of such a God or merit his blessings would be foolish. But faith in the God of the impossible brings hope for the future. God transformed the obstacles Abraham encountered into possibilities for something beyond his dreams. Abraham's faith was not an easy choice; it was a constant struggle. He questioned God, doubted God, pleaded with God. And through this struggle his faith became stronger. For Abraham, the final word was always God's promises (vv. 20–21).

This same God of the impossible was also Paul's God. And Paul convinces us through his writing that this same creating and redeeming God is our God too. The God of Abraham is the God "who raised Jesus our Lord from the dead" (v. 24). The faith of Abraham is a model for all believers— Jews and Gentiles. It is the same faith in the same God who brings the dead to life.

Abraham is the key to understanding the meaning of God's grace and our appropriate response in faith. God's call and promise to Abraham were independent of Abraham's merit or achievement. Justification by grace through faith, creation from nothing, and resurrection from the dead are all affirmations about the same reality. They bear witness to the power of God to evoke new life in situations where there is nothing on which to base hope. The God of the impossible still brings laughter into the world.

After trying to understand Paul's words about Abraham, see if you can answer these questions:

‡ In what ways was faith a struggle for Abraham?

‡ In what ways did Abraham personally experience the God who gives life to the dead and calls into existence what does not exist (v. 17)?

‡ How did Abraham become the "father of us all" (v. 16)?

Meditatio

After thinking about how Paul's words addressed his first readers, reflect on their impact in your own life. After bringing God's Word into the present context of your life, spend some time meditating on these questions:

✝ God transformed the obstacles Abraham encountered into possibilities for something beyond his dreams. How has God transformed the obstacles of my life into something I had never imagined?

✝ In what ways do justification through faith, creation from nothing, and resurrection from the dead characterize the God of the impossible (v. 17)? How does God manifest himself to me as the God of the impossible?

✝ Often it is easier to be paid for something we have earned rather than accept the generosity of God. Why is faith such a struggle for me?

Oratio

We have been justified through the faith of Christ, who, like Abraham, trusted and obeyed God as he listened to his call. Speak to God in union with the faith of Christ.

Creating and redeeming God, you create out of nothing and raise the dead to life. I thank you for offering me the gift of salvation, not through my own merits but through Christ, "who was handed over to death for our trespasses and was raised for our justification."

Continue speaking to God through the grace of Christ . . .

Contemplatio

Place yourself in God's hands through the power of the Holy Spirit. Contemplate the power of God working within you to evoke new life.

Write a few words that arise from your contemplative experience of God's power at work within you.

Operatio

God's power at work within us can do more than we can hope or imagine. How is God working within me today to bring faith out of confusion, hope out of doubt, life out of death?

25

Remembering the Covenant of Old

Kiss the words of the biblical text and ask God to let the inspired words speak powerfully to your spirit today.

LUKE 1:57–75

⁵⁷Now the time came for Elizabeth to give birth, and she bore a son. ⁵⁸Her neighbors and relatives heard that the Lord had shown his great mercy to her, and they rejoiced with her.

⁵⁹On the eighth day they came to circumcise the child, and they were going to name him Zechariah after his father. ⁶⁰But his mother said, "No; he is to be called John." ⁶¹They said to her, "None of your relatives has this name." ⁶²Then they began motioning to his father to find out what name he wanted to give him. ⁶³He asked for a writing tablet and wrote, "His name is John." And all of them were amazed. ⁶⁴Immediately his mouth was opened and his tongue freed, and he began to speak, praising God. ⁶⁵Fear came over all their neighbors, and all these things were talked about throughout the entire hill country of Judea. ⁶⁶All who heard them pondered them and said, "What then will this child become?" For, indeed, the hand of the Lord was with him.

⁶⁷Then his father Zechariah was filled with the Holy Spirit and spoke this prophecy:

> ⁶⁸"Blessed be the Lord God of Israel,
>> for he has looked favorably on his people and redeemed them.
> ⁶⁹He has raised up a mighty savior for us
>> in the house of his servant David,
> ⁷⁰as he spoke through the mouth of his holy prophets from of old,
>> ⁷¹that we would be saved from our enemies and from the hand of all who hate us.
> ⁷²Thus he has shown the mercy promised to our ancestors,
>> and has remembered his holy covenant,
> ⁷³the oath that he swore to our ancestor Abraham,
>> to grant us ⁷⁴that we, being rescued from the hands of our enemies,
> might serve him without fear, ⁷⁵in holiness and righteousness
>> before him all our days.

After carefully listening to this Gospel narrative, continue exploring its meaning in light of the new covenant.

The Gospel according to Luke proclaims that God has remembered his covenant and has kept the promises he made long ago to Abraham. In Jesus, a new period of God's saving plan has begun. This new age of salvation in Jesus Christ is the fulfillment of what God had in mind from ages past, the completion of a pattern God had begun in Abraham almost two thousand years before. What had begun with one person in Abraham was destined to be experienced by all people as the gospel spreads to the east, west, north, and south and breaks down barriers that divide people—Jew and Gentile, rich and poor, man and woman, mighty and humble.

The canticle of Zechariah, the father of John the Baptist, is a programmatic prophecy (vv. 67–75). It is a summary of what God is about to do through the coming of Jesus into the world, and it guides the readers' understanding through the narrative that follows. The prophecy draws heavily from Old Testament texts and prophetic allusions to indicate the continuity of God's plan throughout the generations.

It is significant that the covenant of God with Abraham, "the oath that he swore to our ancestor Abraham" (v. 73), is more fundamental than the covenant with Moses. For Luke, the first Christians are the "descendants of Abraham," through whom the blessings are delivered. Luke makes this clear in his writings in Acts by quoting from the speech of Peter to the believers in Jerusalem: "You are the descendants of the prophets and of the covenant that God gave to your ancestors, saying to Abraham, 'And in your descendants all the families of the earth shall be blessed'" (Acts 3:25).

The occasion of Zechariah's canticle is the circumcision of his son John on the eighth day after his birth (v. 59). How fitting for Zechariah to celebrate "the oath that [God] swore to our ancestor Abraham" (v. 73) at that event! God had first revealed the sign of circumcision to Abraham, who performed the ritual on his sons. The infant John, who would be the prophet called to announce the arrival of the Messiah, was initiated into the ancient faith of Israel and would live his whole life in dedication to that covenant.

The elderly Zechariah and Elizabeth, like their ancestors Abraham and Sarah from so long before, had been living their later life in hopelessness because of their childless state. Yet they were miraculously blessed by God with a child. Again "the Lord God of Israel" has "looked favorably on his people" (v. 68). What God had done at the beginning of salvation history in Abraham and Sarah was now unfolding again as a new age began.

The other programmatic prophecy of Luke's first chapter is Mary's canticle. The Gospel of Luke is about how God reverses destinies: bringing down the powerful and lifting the lowly, filling the hungry with blessings and sending the rich away empty. All of this is "according to the promise he made to our ancestors, to Abraham and to his descendants forever" (v. 55).

After listening to the Gospel text with the ears of your heart, answer this question:

✝ In what ways are the first couple of salvation history (Abraham and Sarah) like the first couple of the New Testament (Zechariah and Elizabeth)?

Meditatio

Imagine what you would see, hear, smell, taste, and feel in this Gospel scene. Place yourself within the scene and ponder its significance for the characters involved.

‡ How does the canticle of Zechariah indicate the continuity of God's saving plan, from Abraham to the coming of Christ?

‡ What is God demonstrating in bringing fertility and birth to elderly and barren couples? In what ways am I barren and in need of new birth?

‡ How does Luke indicate that the first Christians are the descendants of Abraham and heirs of God's covenant with Abraham? In what way am I included in Luke's understanding of God's plan?

Oratio

Recite or chant the words of the canticle as an offering to God.

> Blessed are you, Lord God of Israel. You have looked with favor on your people and proven yourself faithful to your covenant of old. You raised up a mighty Savior for us in your Son Jesus. May I serve you in holiness and righteousness all my days.

Continue to pray in whatever words arise from your own heart...

Contemplatio

Choose a word or phrase from Zechariah's canticle to help you continue to focus on God's presence with you. Realize that your own life is part of God's grand narrative, extending from Abraham to the glorious end of time.

After your time of quiet, choose a few words that express the fruits of your silent contemplation.

Operatio

Zechariah's life was transformed through the Word of God delivered to him. In what way am I being formed and changed through this Gospel text?

26

Father Abraham, Have Mercy on Me

Lectio

Read this parable of Jesus as if for the first time. Hear it as a personal message to you.

LUKE 16:19–31

¹⁹"There was a rich man who was dressed in purple and fine linen and who feasted sumptuously every day. ²⁰And at his gate lay a poor man named Lazarus, covered with sores, ²¹who longed to satisfy his hunger with what fell from the rich man's table; even the dogs would come and lick his sores. ²²The poor man died and was carried away by the angels to be with Abraham. The rich man also died and was buried. ²³In Hades, where he was being tormented, he looked up and saw Abraham far away with Lazarus by his side. ²⁴He called out, 'Father Abraham, have mercy on me, and send Lazarus to dip the tip of his finger in water and cool my tongue; for I am in agony in these flames.' ²⁵But Abraham said, 'Child, remember that during your lifetime you received your good things, and Lazarus in like manner evil things; but now he is comforted here, and you are in agony. ²⁶Besides all this, between you and us a great chasm has been fixed,

so that those who might want to pass from here to you cannot do so, and no one can cross from there to us.' ²⁷He said, 'Then, father, I beg you to send him to my father's house—²⁸for I have five brothers—that he may warn them, so that they will not also come into this place of torment.' ²⁹Abraham replied, 'They have Moses and the prophets; they should listen to them.' ³⁰He said, 'No, father Abraham; but if someone goes to them from the dead, they will repent.' ³¹He said to him, 'If they do not listen to Moses and the prophets, neither will they be convinced even if someone rises from the dead.'"

After listening carefully to these words of Jesus, think about their meaning and significance through this commentary.

The narratives of Abraham in Genesis contain dramatic accounts of how God reverses the human condition: blessing the barren with fertility, bringing an heir to the childless, blessing the outcast slave in the wilderness, rescuing from imminent death. The Gospel of Luke, too, is filled with dramatic reversals: bringing down the powerful, lifting up the lowly, filling the hungry with blessings, sending the rich away empty.

This parable of Jesus continues this theme of reversals. The situations of the rich man and Lazarus could not be more starkly contrasted. The rich man dressed in the finest clothing and feasted sumptuously, not just on special occasions but "every day" (v. 19). The poor man was covered with ulcerated sores and lay among the dogs. Starving, he longed to eat the scraps that fell from the table of the rich man (vv. 20–21). Lazarus lay at the gate of the rich man's home, so evidently the rich man passed him by each day without notice or concern.

Both men died: the poor man obviously from starvation and disease, the rich man probably from conditions that afflict those who feast habitually on rich foods and strong drink. But in the next life their conditions are dramatically reversed. The rich man ends up in torment, and the poor man resides at the side of Abraham (vv. 22–23). The one who failed to show mercy in his earthly life now begs for mercy from "Father Abraham" (v. 24). Not only are their roles reversed, but they are intensified. Abraham's reply sums up the dramatic turnaround: the one who received good things during his lifetime is in "agony" in the afterlife, while the one who received evil things on earth is "comforted" in Abraham's embrace (v. 25). The rich man's agony far exceeds the misery poor Lazarus had ever experienced in life, while the bliss of Lazarus far exceeds the pleasure the rich man had ever experienced.

According to Jewish midrash, Abraham will sit at the entrance to hell to make sure no circumcised Israelite is cast in. He has the authority to rescue them and receive them into heaven. With these legends in mind, the rich man believed that Abraham would give him comfort by sending Lazarus either to bring him a drop of cool water or warn his five brothers to repent (vv. 24, 27–28). But, as John the Baptist has already indicated, it is not enough to claim "we have Abraham as our ancestor." Rather, the children of Abraham must "bear fruits worthy of repentance" (Luke 3:8).

The rich man's neglect of the poor man at his gate was a clear rejection of "Moses and the prophets" (v. 29). The law of Moses demanded, "If there is among you anyone in need, . . . do not be hard-hearted or tight-fisted toward your needy neighbor" (Deut. 15:7). Likewise, the prophets do not relent: "Share your bread with the hungry, and bring the homeless poor into your house" (Isa. 58:7). Abraham declared, finally, that if the rich man's brothers do not listen to Moses and the prophets, they will not be convinced "even if someone rises from the dead" (v. 31). Those who refuse to obey the clear words of the Scriptures will also reject the message of the risen Christ.

After grappling with the message of this parable, test your understanding by answering these questions:

✝ What does this parable indicate to be a determining factor for entry into heaven?

✝ What seems to be the role of Abraham in this parable of Jesus?

Meditatio

Allow the words of the parable to interact with your own world of ideas, concerns, thoughts, and feelings. Ask yourself what the text means to you.

✝ Since the rich man and his brothers have the clear teachings of the Scriptures, what is their problem? When do I have similar problems in grasping the meaning of Scripture?

✝ Which words of this parable have the most impact on me? What parts of the parable make me uncomfortable?

✝ The biblical story, from beginning to end, seems to be a series of reversals. How does this reality help me understand the meaning of the Christian life?

Oratio

Speak to God in response to the words, ideas, and images of the Gospel text. Respond to the One who knows you intimately, cares about you deeply, and accepts you unconditionally.

> God of Abraham and Father of Jesus, you are the God of the living and the dead. May I live my life in such a way as to give glory to you. Give me a compassionate heart so that I will notice and heed the needs of those around me.

Continue speaking to God in whatever ways seem to respond to the divine Word spoken to you . . .

Contemplatio

Imagine God's immense and steadfast love for the hungry and poor. Try to contemplate the world around you with the caring eyes and the compassionate heart of Christ.

Write a few words about your contemplative experience.

Operatio

Does my life more closely resemble that of the rich man or of Lazarus? Who are the needy at my gate? What can I do to help them?

27

Doing What Abraham Did

Listen to these challenging words of Jesus as he speaks to early hearers of his message and to you. Highlight the words that you find most difficult to hear and to obey.

JOHN 8:31–42

³¹Then Jesus said to the Jews who had believed in him, "If you continue in my word, you are truly my disciples; ³²and you will know the truth, and the truth will make you free." ³³They answered him, "We are descendants of Abraham and have never been slaves to anyone. What do you mean by saying, 'You will be made free'?"

³⁴Jesus answered them, "Very truly, I tell you, everyone who commits sin is a slave to sin. ³⁵The slave does not have a permanent place in the household; the son has a place there forever. ³⁶So if the Son makes you free, you will be free indeed. ³⁷I know that you are descendants of Abraham; yet you look for an opportunity to kill me, because there is no place in you for my word. ³⁸I declare what I have seen in the Father's presence; as for you, you should do what you have heard from the Father."

³⁹They answered him, "Abraham is our father." Jesus said to them, "If you were Abraham's children, you would be doing what Abraham

did, [40]but now you are trying to kill me, a man who has told you the truth that I heard from God. This is not what Abraham did. [41]You are indeed doing what your father does." They said to him, "We are not illegitimate children; we have one father, God himself." [42]Jesus said to them, "If God were your Father, you would love me, for I came from God and now I am here. I did not come on my own, but he sent me.

Continue listening to the teachings of Jesus as they are understood through the tradition of his church.

The dialogue between Jesus and those Jews who have taken a hostile position toward him revolves around the question of paternity: Who is our father? To be a child of a father means listening to the words of that father and doing what he does. What does it mean to be a child of Abraham? Is it a matter of physical descent, or something more? If God is our Father, what does that imply? Surely children of the same father would love one another.

Jesus proclaimed that by believing in his Word, his disciples would know the truth, and that truth would set them free (vv. 31–32). His antagonists, however, proclaimed that they are descendants of Abraham, and as Abraham's posterity they have always been spiritually free and never slaves (v. 33). Jesus responded that it is sin that makes us slaves and prevents us from having a secure place in God's household (vv. 34–35). To have a permanent place in the household, we must be children of God, a status we receive through believing the Word of Jesus and coming to know the truth. The freedom that results from this personal acceptance of the saving Word of Jesus is a deep confidence and interior freedom that results from an intimate relationship with God (v. 36).

Resisting the invitation of Jesus, his listeners claim, "Abraham is our father" (v. 39). Jesus acknowledges that they are physical descendants of Abraham, just as he himself is (v. 37). But bloodline does not determine genuine sonship and freedom. True children do what their father does. If they were true children of Abraham, they "would be doing what Abraham did" (v. 39). Unlike Abraham, they have not opened their lives to the transforming power of God's Word. Abraham was a man of faith, from his response to God's call to leave his homeland to his willingness to offer his son to God. When God sent the divine messengers to Abraham (Gen. 18), the faithful patriarch welcomed them. But the opponents of Jesus have rejected the Word of God made known in Jesus, the heavenly messenger, and are trying to kill him (v. 40).

Jesus teaches that there is no contradiction between being a child of Abraham and a child of God. All who listen to God like Abraham and respond in action to God's Word are truly Abraham's descendants. And all these children of Abraham are free children of God, living permanently in the household of God. Indeed, Israel is described in the Scriptures as God's firstborn son (Exod. 4:22). Since Jesus is from God and beloved of God, surely all those who have God as their Father should accept the one sent from God. Children of the same Father should love one another (vv. 41–42).

After seeking to understand the exchange between Jesus and his opponents in this scene, answer these questions:

‡ What indicates that the opponents of Jesus are not living as children of Abraham?

‡ Who are the true descendants of Abraham? What is required to be identified as a child of Abraham?

‡ How do people become children of God? What are the effects of being God's children?

Meditatio

Ask yourself how Jesus is speaking to you in this passage and how you can respond with obedience.

‡ Jesus taught, "You will know the truth, and the truth will make you free" (v. 32). What is the practical meaning of this verse in my own life?

‡ Does my life indicate that I am a child of Abraham and a child of God? What are the primary indicators?

‡ In what ways has my faith been communicated to me through my family tree? Why is receiving faith from my ancestors not enough to make me a child of my Father's household?

Oratio

Acknowledge before God the ways you are in bondage to sin and pray in the freedom of knowing that God is your Father.

Lord Jesus, open my ears to hear your Word and open my heart to accept it. Remove from my life all that would distort your Word so that I can experience the freedom that comes from living in your truth.

Continue to pray in response to the Word you have heard . . .

Contemplatio

Rest in the assurance that you are a child of Abraham and a child of God. Trust that God knows you intimately and loves you without measure.

Write a few words that linger from your silent time in God's presence.

Operatio

How is God forming me as his child as I respond to his Word? What new hope and renewed sense of mission have I received from my lectio divina?

28

Greater than
Our Father Abraham

Lectio

As Jesus continues this discourse with his opponents, listen to his challenging and encouraging words. Read the words of the dialogue aloud to
heighten their impact.

JOHN 8:48–59

⁴⁸The Jews answered him, "Are we not right in saying that you are
a Samaritan and have a demon?" ⁴⁹Jesus answered, "I do not have a
demon; but I honor my Father, and you dishonor me. ⁵⁰Yet I do not
seek my own glory; there is one who seeks it and he is the judge. ⁵¹Very
truly, I tell you, whoever keeps my word will never see death." ⁵²The
Jews said to him, "Now we know that you have a demon. Abraham
died, and so did the prophets; yet you say, 'Whoever keeps my word
will never taste death.' ⁵³Are you greater than our father Abraham,
who died? The prophets also died. Who do you claim to be?" ⁵⁴Jesus
answered, "If I glorify myself, my glory is nothing. It is my Father
who glorifies me, he of whom you say, 'He is our God,' ⁵⁵though
you do not know him. But I know him; if I would say that I do not
know him, I would be a liar like you. But I do know him and I keep

his word. ⁵⁶Your ancestor Abraham rejoiced that he would see my day; he saw it and was glad." ⁵⁷Then the Jews said to him, "You are not yet fifty years old, and have you seen Abraham?" ⁵⁸Jesus said to them, "Very truly, I tell you, before Abraham was, I am." ⁵⁹So they picked up stones to throw at him, but Jesus hid himself and went out of the temple.

Let the words of Jesus continue to impact your heart as you seek their full significance through this commentary.

Having proclaimed that continuing in his Word brings knowledge of the truth and genuine freedom (vv. 31–32), Jesus proclaims another astonishing promise: "Whoever keeps my word will never see death" (v. 51). Abiding in the Word of Jesus, living out its demands, taking it to heart, leads to a life that lasts forever.

Again the words of Jesus are rejected by his opponents with an appeal to Abraham (vv. 52–53). Surely, they say, Jesus could not be greater than their father Abraham. Abraham and all the prophets after him died; how can Jesus offer eternal life?

Jesus counters his opponents' appeal to Abraham with an appeal to God himself, the supreme Life-giver (vv. 54–55). Though the Jews who have taken a hostile position toward Jesus claim they are children of Abraham, Jesus says that Abraham accepted God's designs while they do not. Abraham rejoiced that he was to see the day of Jesus (v. 56), while they do not. Abraham looked forward to the accomplishments of God in the new age. He believed God's promise that through his offspring blessings would eventually come to the whole world (Gen. 12:3). From this biblical promise came a Jewish rabbinical tradition that Abraham had been given a revelation of the secrets of the age to come, especially the age of the Messiah. For this reason, Jesus claimed that Abraham foresaw the time of Jesus and was glad.

Asked how Jesus could possibly have seen Abraham since Jesus lived almost two millennia after Abraham's lifetime, Jesus responded with the most amazing claim yet: "Very truly, I tell you, before Abraham was, I am" (v. 58). The Son of God, the Word of God, was already in existence from the beginning. The opening words of John's Gospel, evoking the opening words of Genesis, had proclaimed, "In the beginning was the Word" (John 1:1). Existing from eternity, Jesus transcends time. He speaks with the voice of the God of Abraham, Isaac, and Jacob, the God of the living. He is the source of life and hope even for Abraham and all the prophets. This claim to divinity was too much for the crowd who rejected his message, and they took up stones to cast at this blasphemer.

After hearing this exchange between Jesus and his listeners, answer these questions about the text:

✝ What is necessary, according to Jesus, to experience life that does not end?

✝ What is the essence of Jesus's response to his opponents' question: "Are you greater than our father Abraham?" (v. 53).

✝ Could there be a relationship between the solemn proclamation of Jesus in verse 58 and the words of God to Moses in Exodus 3:14?

✝ Why does this final claim of Jesus (v. 58) cause such an outrage?

Meditatio

Repeat and ponder whatever words strike you most from your lectio. Reflect on how God is deepening your understanding and enriching your hope for the future.

✝ How does Jesus fulfill God's promises to Abraham? How does he fulfill God's promises to me?

✝ What are the deepest hopes of all people? What assures me that I can entrust my future to Jesus?

✝ Of the three solemn claims made by Jesus in this encounter (vv. 32, 51, 58), which strikes me the most strongly and offers me the most hope?

Oratio

Having listened and reflected on God's Word to you in the Gospel text, now respond to God from your heart in prayer.

Divine Lord, you are the hope of Israel and of all the nations of the earth. Let your Word penetrate my heart, make me secure in your promises, and lead me to eternal life.

Continue praying in whatever words seem to express the content of your heart . . .

Contemplatio

Jesus has given you promises of freedom and life. God's intimate knowledge of you and God's eternal plan for your life are too wonderful to understand. Rest in the wonder of God's care for you.

What words come to mind after your contemplative time in God's presence?

Operatio

What practical difference does God's assurance of freedom and eternal life make in my life today? How do I live differently, knowing that my life will not come to an end?

29

The Line of Abraham's Descendants

Read aloud the speech of Stephen before his martyrdom. Listen to his words as if you were among the crowd in Jerusalem in the church's earliest days.

ACTS 7:1–8

[1]Then the high priest asked him, "Are these things so?" [2]And Stephen replied: "Brothers and fathers, listen to me. The God of glory appeared to our ancestor Abraham when he was in Mesopotamia, before he lived in Haran, [3]and said to him, 'Leave your country and your relatives and go to the land that I will show you.' [4]Then he left the country of the Chaldeans and settled in Haran. After his father died, God had him move from there to this country in which you are now living. [5]He did not give him any of it as a heritage, not even a foot's length, but promised to give it to him as his possession and to his descendants after him, even though he had no child. [6]And God spoke in these terms, that his descendants would be resident aliens in a country belonging to others, who would enslave them and mistreat them during four hundred years. [7]'But I will judge the nation that they serve,' said God, 'and after that they shall come out and worship me in this place.' [8]Then he gave him

the covenant of circumcision. And so Abraham became the father of Isaac and circumcised him on the eighth day; and Isaac became the father of Jacob, and Jacob of the twelve patriarchs.

Continue seeking to understand the significance of Abraham's life in the context of Christian discipleship.

The arrest, speech, and martyrdom of Stephen (Acts 6–7) is a turning point in the early days of the church in Jerusalem, as narrated in the Acts of the Apostles. His death and the ensuing persecution launched the church's expansion to the surrounding regions and eventually into the whole world (8:1).

After being arrested, Stephen was falsely charged with speaking blasphemous words against God, Moses, and the temple, claiming that Jesus would destroy the temple and change the law of Moses (6:11–14). When the high priest asked Stephen, "Are these things so" (v. 1), Stephen began the longest and one of the most important speeches in the Acts of the Apostles. Through Stephen's words, the author provides the reader with an interpretation of the entire two-volume work (the Gospel of Luke and the Acts of the Apostles). Covering a huge amount of the biblical story with great compression, Stephen recounts the history of salvation, beginning with Abraham and continuing through Moses, David, Solomon, and the construction of the temple. The purpose of this survey is to demonstrate that this saving history is continued in Jesus and the apostles.

The subject of the speech is clearly God. He is called "the God of glory" (v. 2). This divine title suggests the manifestation of God's presence on earth, which came to be known as the "Shekinah." This glory of God was associated primarily with the tent of God's dwelling in the wilderness and then with the temple in Jerusalem. But Stephen declares that God needs neither tent nor temple, for God manifested himself to Abraham while he was still living in Mesopotamia and was present with him throughout all his wanderings.

The first part of Stephen's speech is about what God has done in Abraham. God is the actor: God appeared to Abraham (v. 2); God spoke to him (vv. 3, 6); God showed Abraham the land; God had Abraham move to Canaan (v. 4); God promised (v. 5); God judged (v. 7); and God gave Abraham the covenant (v. 8). Stephen's emphasis is on what God has done in the past and promised for the future. Those promises of God are fulfilled in surprising ways throughout Israel's history, namely through the exodus from slavery and entry into the Promised Land (vv. 6–7). But Stephen's primary point is that what God began in Abraham continues into the history of Jesus and his church. The promises to Abraham are being fulfilled in the messianic mission of Jesus Christ.

At the time of Luke's writing, the many factions within Judaism were competing over who was the legitimate successor to the ancient history of Israel. With the temple destroyed by the Romans (AD 70), the debate within the family of Judaism is over who will continue the family line, who can lay claim to authentic family membership. Stephen is in a grueling life-and-death struggle with his fellow Jews over who is the real heir of the family inheritance. Stephen argues that the people of God no longer depend on the temple in Jerusalem, nor are they ruled by the high priest and his council. Rather, they are those who inherit the promises made to Abraham through participating in their fulfillment in the Good News of Jesus Christ. In response to Stephen's long and pivotal speech, his antagonists dragged him outside the city gates and stoned him to death for blasphemy.

After listening to the courageous words of Stephen, think about these questions:

‡ Why is it important for followers of Jesus to be able to summarize the history of God's saving deeds from Abraham to Jesus?

‡ What is the main point of Stephen's speech? In what way is it a turning point in Luke's narrative history of the early church?

Meditatio

Spend some time meditating on the fact that your life is now a part of the sacred history of Israel because you live in Christ. Reflect on this amazing story of salvation from Abraham to Jesus.

‡ Given the fact that the high priest and Stephen know the same history of Abraham and Israel, what might be the reason for their drastically different responses to Jesus?

‡ How do the stories of Abraham convince me that God's presence cannot be confined to a particular place? Where do I most clearly experience the manifestation of God?

‡ In what way are the promises made to Abraham fulfilled in Jesus? In what way are they fulfilled in my life? How do I know that God is faithful?

Oratio

Pray for a gift of courage like Stephen's and for the ability to evangelize others through the witness of your Christian faith.

Risen Lord, in you all the nations of the earth are blessed and all people can respond to the Good News of your saving death and resurrection. Bless me with strong faith so that I might be a witness for you.

Continue to pray as the Holy Spirit prompts you . . .

Contemplatio

When words are no longer necessary or helpful in your prayer, just remain in quiet to appreciate the presence of "the God of glory" (v. 2) within you. Know that God is working within you to deepen your faith and transform your heart through your openness to the divine presence.

Write a few words to describe your time of contemplatio.

Operatio

Think about how to be a more effective sign of God's presence in the world. How can I be a witness for Christ today in my public life?

30

The Example of
Abraham's Faith

Ask the Holy Spirit to open your eyes, ears, and heart as the inspired text proclaims the faith of Abraham and informs your faith.

HEBREWS 11:8–19

⁸By faith Abraham obeyed when he was called to set out for a place that he was to receive as an inheritance; and he set out, not knowing where he was going. ⁹By faith he stayed for a time in the land he had been promised, as in a foreign land, living in tents, as did Isaac and Jacob, who were heirs with him of the same promise. ¹⁰For he looked forward to the city that has foundations, whose architect and builder is God. ¹¹By faith he received power of procreation, even though he was too old—and Sarah herself was barren—because he considered him faithful who had promised. ¹²Therefore from one person, and this one as good as dead, descendants were born, "as many as the stars of heaven and as the innumerable grains of sand by the seashore."

¹³All of these died in faith without having received the promises, but from a distance they saw and greeted them. They confessed that they were strangers and foreigners on the earth, ¹⁴for people who speak in this way make it clear that they are seeking a homeland. ¹⁵If they had

been thinking of the land that they had left behind, they would have had opportunity to return. [16]But as it is, they desire a better country, that is, a heavenly one. Therefore God is not ashamed to be called their God; indeed, he has prepared a city for them.

[17]By faith Abraham, when put to the test, offered up Isaac. He who had received the promises was ready to offer up his only son, [18]of whom he had been told, "It is through Isaac that descendants shall be named for you." [19]He considered the fact that God is able even to raise someone from the dead—and figuratively speaking, he did receive him back.

After slowly listening to this inspired passage, continue your struggle to understand its meaning and its significance.

Above all his many qualities, Abraham is best known for his faith. According to Genesis, "he believed the LORD; and the LORD reckoned it to him as righteousness" (Gen. 15:6). Paul described Abraham as "the ancestor of all who believe" (Rom. 4:11). "Those who believe are blessed with Abraham who believed" (Gal. 3:9). In the letter to the Hebrews, the writer holds up the life of Abraham as a model of faith, highlighting three major chapters in his life.

First of all, Abraham was sent by God on a journey of faith. Abraham obeyed and departed, not knowing where he was going, trusting only that God would give him the land as an inheritance (v. 8). He left the known and familiar and entrusted his future to God. Reaching the Promised Land, he continued to journey in tents, like a stranger in a foreign land (v. 9). A man of faith, Abraham was utterly dependant on God and motivated only by God's promises.

The second illustration of Abraham's faith was his trusting belief in God's promises of descendants. Abraham was promised what was humanly impossible. Though he was most likely impotent and Sarah was barren, God promised Abraham that he would have descendants in abundance (vv. 11–12). Abraham and Sarah received the power of procreation because they trusted in the faithfulness and trustworthiness of God.

The last example of Abraham's faith was the testing involved in the offering of Isaac. Abraham's faith in God was so strong that "he considered the fact that God is able even to raise someone from the dead" (vv. 17–19). God's act of saving Isaac from death was as though God had raised him from the dead. Yet, the allusion goes beyond Isaac to the anticipation of Christ. Like Abraham, God willingly offered his only Son, whom he raised from the dead through the resurrection. Belief in the power of God to raise the dead to life is the greatest faith.

The chapters of Abraham's life demonstrate the faith defined by the author of Hebrews: "Faith is the assurance of things hoped for, the conviction of things not seen" (11:1). Abraham was the pilgrim traveler—journeying toward the unseen and the unknown, acting on the basis of God's promises alone. The things hoped for guided his life, though he died without having received the promises (v. 13). He spent his life reaching for what he only glimpsed in the distance.

The promises and blessings experienced by Abraham, as wonderful as they were, were only a shadow of the transcendent reality still to come. Like all of us, he knew that his true "homeland" was not to be found in his earthly life (v. 14). The Promised Land was only a tract of real estate on the eastern shore of the Mediterranean. Abraham looked forward to "a better country" (v. 16), to "the city that has foundations," a stable and lasting city "whose architect and builder is God" (v. 10).

Abraham's faith was not a passive waiting; it was a lively obedience and active pilgrimage motivated by God's trustworthiness. As James explained in his letter, Abraham's faith was brought to completion by his works (James 2:21–24). God's promises, the things hoped for, though not yet seen, are a powerful motivator for people of faith. Like Abraham, we live our lives as traveling pilgrims, not always knowing where we are going but led by God's promises. The journey is never confined to one generation, it is in opposition to the demands of our culture that wants everything now, and it is always challenging and risky. Abraham, the father of all believers, has gone ahead of us to show us the way. As his children from among all the nations, may we be blessed through him.

Meditatio

Consider how this summary of Abraham's life of faith relates to your own experiences of faith in God.

‡ How does Abraham's life illustrate the definition of faith given in Hebrews 11:1? In what ways is Abraham a model of faith for me?

‡ What obstacles did Abraham have to overcome in each of the three episodes that defined his faith? What three chapters of my life have best demonstrated the challenges of faith?

‡ How would the world be different if all the descendants of Abraham realized they are "strangers and foreigners on the earth" (v. 13) seeking a common "homeland" (v. 14)?

Oratio

Address your prayer to the God and Father of all people. Ask God to bless and guide the sons and daughters of Abraham throughout the world on the road to peace.

God of Abraham, you have called us to be traveling pilgrims on the earth and have assured us that you are faithful to your promises. May we join with all the sons and daughters of Abraham as we journey together toward our final homeland with you.

Continue to implore God with trusting faith in his will . . .

Contemplatio

Entrust your hopes for God's people and for our world into the hands of our Creator and Redeemer. Ask to experience the peace that comes from God.

Write a few words to conclude your time of peaceful contemplation.

Operatio

How has this study of Abraham shaped and changed me? How can I partner with God to help penetrate the world with the healing news of Abraham's God, the Father of all believers?

Ancient-Future Bible Study for Small Groups

A small group for *collatio*, the communal practice of lectio divina, is a wonderful way to let the power of Scripture more deeply nourish participants. Through the thoughts, reflections, prayers, and experiences of the other members of the group, each individual comes to understand Scripture more intensely and experience it more profoundly. By sharing our understanding and wisdom in a faith-filled group of people, we discover how to let God live in every dimension of our lives and we enrich the lives of others.

These groups may be formed in any number of ways, just as you create groups for other learning experiences within your community. Groups composed of no more than a dozen people are best for this experience. It is preferable to give people with various needs a variety of days and times from which to choose.

Small groups are best formed when people are encouraged and supported by a church's pastoral leadership and personally welcomed into these small communities. Personally directed invitations are most effective for convincing people to add another dimension to their schedules.

The collatio should never take the place of one's regular, personal lectio divina. Rather, a weekly communal practice is an ideal extension and continuation of personal, daily sacred reading. At each group session, participants discuss the fruits of their individual lectio divina and practice elements of lectio divina together.

Participants should read carefully the opening sections of this book before joining the group. "The Movements of Lectio Divina," "The Essence of Lectio Divina," and "Your Personal Practice of Ancient-Future Bible Study" would be helpful sections to review throughout the course of the study.

The full weekly collatio group session is designed for about ninety minutes. Those groups with limited time may choose either Part 1 or Part 2 for the group experience. Instructions for each of the collatio groups are provided on the following pages.

Suggestions for Participating in the Group

‡ The spirit of the collatio should be that of a personal conversation, with the members desiring to learn from one another and building each other up. The divine Word is the teacher; the members of the group are all learners.

‡ When participating in the group, members should offer their thoughts, insights, and feelings about the sacred text. The group can avoid the distraction of off-topic chatter by sticking to the text, the commentary, and their personal response to the text from the meditatio.

‡ Group members should be careful to give everyone in the group an opportunity to share. When discussing personal thoughts, members should use "I" language and be cautious about giving advice to others. They should listen attentively to the other members of the group so as to learn from their insights and should not worry about trying to cover all the questions in each gathering. They should select only those that seem the most helpful for group discussion.

‡ Dispute, debate, and dogmatic hairsplitting within the group erode its focus and purpose. Opposition and division destroy the supportive bond of the group. The desire of individuals to assert themselves and their own ideas wears down the spirit of the group. In a community setting, it is often wise to "agree to disagree." An inflexible, pedantic attitude blocks the way to a vital and fulfilling understanding of the passage. The Scriptures are the living Word of God, the full meaning of which we can never exhaust.

‡ It is usually helpful to have someone to guide the process of the group. This facilitator directs the discussion, helping the group keep the discussion on time and on track. The facilitator need not be an expert, either in Scripture or in the process of lectio divina, but simply a person with the skills necessary to guide a group. This role may be rotated among members of the group, if desired.

Group Study
in Six Sessions

✝ Begin each group session with hospitality and welcome. Name tags are helpful if group members don't know one another. Offer any announcements or instructions before entering the spirit of prayer.

✝ Set the tone and focus the group by saying the gathering prayer together.

✝ Note that the first group session is a bit different from the others because it involves reading and discussing the introduction. After the first group session, all the remaining sessions follow the same format.

✝ The group sessions are in two parts. Part 1 is a discussion of the fruits of the lectio divina that participants completed on their own since the last group session. To provoke personal discussion of each chapter, ask this question: "What insight is most significant to you from your reflection on this chapter?" Group members may mention insights they gained in the lectio, meditatio, oratio, contemplatio, or operatio of each chapter.

✝ Part 2 is a session of lectio divina in the group. Leave at least half of the group time for this section. Move through each of the five movements as described in the chapter. Read the text aloud, followed by the commentary. Leave the most time for the more personal questions of the meditatio. Don't worry if you don't complete them all.

✝ Leave sufficient time for the oratio, contemplatio, and operatio. These movements should not be rushed. Gently guide the group from vocal prayer into a period of restful silence. Don't neglect to conclude the lectio divina by mentioning some practical fruits of operatio before dismissing the group into the world of daily discipleship.

✝ Conclude each group session by encouraging participants to complete the lectio divina on their own for the upcoming chapters. Ask them to write their responses to each movement of lectio in their book.

Collatio Group 1

✝ The first group session is a bit different from the others. After offering greetings and introductions, explain the process of Ancient-Future Bible Study. Then set the tone for the group experience by praying together the gathering prayer.

✝ Gathering prayer:

> *Come upon us, Holy Spirit, to enlighten and guide us as we begin this study of Abraham. You inspired the writers of Scripture to reveal your presence throughout the history of salvation. This inspired Word has the power to convert our hearts and change our lives. Fill our hearts with desire, trust, and confidence as you shine the light of your truth within us. Motivate us to read the Scriptures and give us a deeper love for God's Word each day. Bless us during this session and throughout the coming week with the fire of your love.*

✝ Spend the first half of the collatio group reading the introduction to this book and discussing the questions to consider. A volunteer may read each section aloud, and the group will spend a few minutes discussing the questions that follow.

✝ Spend the second half of the group time following the five movements of the lectio divina at the end of the introduction. Read the text aloud, followed by the commentary. Then spend time reflecting and sharing responses to the questions of the meditatio.

✝ When leading into the oratio, pray the prayer aloud, then leave time for additional prayers from the group. When the vocal prayer has receded, lead the group into contemplatio. Help the group to feel comfortable with the quiet and relax in the presence of God. Conclude the lectio divina with the operatio. Share encouragement and commitment to practice lectio divina throughout the week.

✝ Before departing, instruct group members in their practice of lectio divina during the week. Participants should complete the lectio divina for chapters 1–5 for next week. Encourage them to write their responses to each movement of lectio in their book. The lectio divina for chapter 6 will be done together in the group next week.

Collatio Group 2

✝ Gathering prayer:

> *Creating and redeeming God, the life of Abraham offers us a model of renewal and new beginnings, of entrusting the future to you. His life was marked by weaknesses and fears, filled with worries and doubts. Yet, because he trusted you, he was able to make difficult choices in extreme circumstances. Help us to know that you are our Protector and the source of all that we need. Help us to use the gifts you have given us to cultivate a life that gives honor and glory to you.*

✝ Part 1:
- Having completed the lectio divina for chapters 1–5 during the week, the group members discuss the fruit of their practice for these five chapters. Divide the chapters into equal time allotments so that no chapter is neglected. To provoke personal discussion of each chapter, ask this question: "What insight is most significant to you from your reflection on this chapter?"

✝ Part 2:
- Spend at least the last half of the group time in the full lectio divina of chapter 6. Move through each step according to the instructions provided in the chapter, leaving plenty of time for oratio, contemplatio, and operatio.

✝ Departure:
- Encourage participants to complete the lectio divina for chapters 7–11 before the next collatio group. Ask them to write their responses to each movement of lectio in their book. The lectio divina for chapter 12 will be done together in the group next week.

Collatio Group 3

✝ Gathering prayer:

> *God of all creation, you promised an everlasting covenant to Abraham and his descendents. Help us believe that we have inherited the promises you entrusted to our ancestor Abraham.*

When we are besieged by doubts and fears, help us to trust that we await a wondrous fulfillment of what you have pledged to us. Give us an active concern for the people of your world, and encourage us to act as bearers of your covenant in the world today.

‡ Part 1:
  • Having completed the lectio divina for chapters 7–11 during the week, the group members discuss the fruit of their practice for these five chapters. Divide the chapters into equal time allotments so that no chapter is neglected. To provoke personal discussion of each chapter, ask this question: "What insight is most significant to you from your reflection on this chapter?"

‡ Part 2:
  • Spend at least the last half of the group time in the full lectio divina of chapter 12. Move through each step according to the instructions provided in the chapter, leaving plenty of time for oratio, contemplatio, and operatio.

‡ Departure:
  • Encourage participants to complete the lectio divina for chapters 13–17 before the next collatio group. Ask them to write their responses to each movement of lectio in their book. The lectio divina for chapter 18 will be done together in the group next week.

Collatio Group 4

‡ Gathering prayer:

God of our fathers and mothers, in every generation you have tested the faith of your children, but you have also provided for all their needs. Your covenant with us is strengthened through the obedient offering of our lives. Give us your compassion for the outcast and banished people among us, and give us the strength to remain faithful and devoted to the people you have entrusted to us. May we trust in your plan for our lives and become examples of faithful devotion to you for the next generation.

‡ Part 1:
  • Having completed the lectio divina for chapters 13–17 during the week, the group members discuss the fruit of their practice for these five

chapters. Divide the chapters into equal time allotments so that no chapter is neglected. To provoke personal discussion of each chapter, ask this question: "What insight is most significant to you from your reflection on this chapter?"

✝ Part 2:
- Spend at least the last half of the group time in the full lectio divina of chapter 18. Move through each step according to the instructions provided in the chapter, leaving plenty of time for oratio, contemplatio, and operatio.

✝ Departure:
- Encourage participants to complete the lectio divina for chapters 19–23 before the next collatio group. Ask them to write their responses to each movement of lectio in their book. The lectio divina for chapter 24 will be done together in the group next week.

Collatio Group 5

✝ Gathering prayer:

> *Lord our God, we sing your praise and glory in your holy name. You transformed Abraham's obstacles into possibilities beyond his dreams. You have done wonderful works among your people and remembered your covenant with Abraham for a thousand generations. We give you thanks for making us heirs to your covenant through Jesus Christ. We pray for an increase in the gift of faith so that all our actions may be done in union with Jesus your Son.*

✝ Part 1:
- Having completed the lectio divina for chapters 19–23 during the week, the group members discuss the fruit of their practice for these five chapters. Divide the chapters into equal time allotments so that no chapter is neglected. The most effective question to ask of each chapter is this: "What is your most important insight from this chapter?"

✝ Part 2:
- Spend at least the last half of the group time in the full lectio divina of chapter 24. Move through each step according to the instructions

provided in the chapter, leaving plenty of time for oratio, contemplatio, and operatio.

‡ Departure:
- Encourage participants to complete the lectio divina for chapters 25–29 before the next collatio group. Ask them to write their responses to each movement of lectio in their book. The lectio divina for chapter 30 will be done together in the group next week.

Collatio Group 6

‡ Gathering prayer:

> *God of Abraham and Father of Jesus, you have proven your faithfulness to your ancient covenant by sending your Son as Israel's Messiah. In him the numbers of Abraham's children grow beyond counting like the stars in the sky and all the nations of the earth are blessed. Let your Word penetrate our hearts, and bless us with faith like that of Abraham. May we witness to your faithfulness and serve you all our days.*

‡ Part 1:
- Having completed the lectio divina for chapters 25–29 during the week, the group members discuss the fruit of their practice for these five chapters. Divide the chapters into equal time allotments so that no chapter is neglected. The most effective question to ask of each chapter is this: "What is your most important insight from this chapter?"

‡ Part 2:
- Spend at least the last half of the group time in the full lectio divina of chapter 30. Move through each step according to the instructions provided in the chapter, leaving plenty of time for oratio, contemplatio, and operatio.

‡ Departure:
- Discuss how this Ancient-Future Bible Study has made a difference in the lives of group members and whether the group wishes to study another book in the series. Consult www.brazospress.com/ancient futurebiblestudy for more study options.